Where Are You, God?

John Oswalt

While this book is designed for the reader's personal enjoyment, it is also intended for group study. A Leader's Guide with Victor Multiuse Transparency Masters is available from your local bookstore or from the publisher.

VICTOR BOOKS

a division of SP Publications, Inc.

WHEATON. ILLINOIS 60187

Offices also in Fullerton, California • Whitby, Ontario, Canada • Amersham-on-the-Hill, Bucks, England

Recommended Dewey Decimal Classification: 224.99
    Suggested Subject Heading: MALACHI

Library of Congress Catalog Card Number: 81-86528
ISBN: 0-88207-353-2

© 1982 by SP Publications, Inc. All rights reserved
Printed in the United States of America

VICTOR BOOKS
A division of SP Publications, Inc.
P.O. Box 1825 ● Wheaton, Illinois 60187

CONTENTS

For
Karen
Pete and Jean, Willy and Reba
Charles and Beth, Arv and Judy, Ron and Nadara
who will know why

I
THE LOSS
OF GOD

1
WHERE IS GOD?

You have recently been faced with the question of God's justice. We all have. From the senseless rape and murder of a teenage girl in Middle America to the appalling reality of Protestants and Catholics, both professing Christ, bombing each other into oblivion in Northern Ireland, the question crowds in on us daily, "God, where are You? We want to believe in You, but why are there so many unanswered questions?"

Sometimes easy answers only compound the question. On an April night in 1974, two great walls of air, one cold and one warm, slammed into each other somewhere over Kansas. That collision spawned an unheard-of number of tornados, which spun their destructive courses eastward across the South and Midwest. Eyewitnesses reported funnel clouds both north and south of Wilmore, Kentucky, our small town where Asbury Seminary and College are located.

"How like God," we were saying. "He knew we have a great work to do, and 'He tempered the wind to the shorn lamb'!"

You can imagine how unwelcome were the muttered words of the wag who said, "Then I wonder what awful things the residents of Brandenburg have done." You see, Brandenburg, Kentucky was almost totally destroyed. To say *we* were saved by a direct act of God is to say *they* were destroyed by a direct act of God. But were we any more deserving than they?

Why is it that so many Mafia dons live out their lives in the lap of luxury and die in their beds as cherubic old men? Of course, many thugs do come to a bad and desperate end. But something in us cries out that if there is a God in heaven, they *all* ought to end up that way, and they certainly don't.

On the other hand, here is Joe, good and upright, struggling to support a family, intent on doing what is right. His employer is doctoring the company records to dodge the IRS. After a struggle with his conscience and God, Joe suggests in the best way he can that this is wrong. What happens? Joe gets fired.

Human Discouragement

Sometimes the contradictions of the world, with Bangladeshes and Vietnams, become almost too much for a thoughtful and sensitive person to bear. He cries out with Mr. Nickles in Archibald MacLeish's play, *J.B.*, "If God is God, He is not good. If God is good, He is not God." In short, the god who *rules* this world cannot be good or he would not allow evil things to happen.

Samuel Clemens, the famous Mark Twain, was burdened by what he saw as the injustices of life. As he grew older he became more and more embittered. His short story "The Mysterious Stranger" is a heartbreaking picture of Clemens' anger at God. Two boys, walking in a woods, meet a man who proceeds to show them his miraculous powers. He can create miniature people. He does so, and puts his creatures down in a clearing in the forest. The boys watch entranced as the little people build a castle and its surrounding villages. But just at the point where all the prodigious labors seem about to yield their blessings for the people, the stranger fashions an evil-looking storm cloud and sends it scudding across the clearing toward the little civilization. The boys watch with tears streaming down their faces, as the tiny men and women struggle to save themselves and their possessions. The cloudburst and ensuing flood are too much, and destroy everyone and everything. As the boys hurl their reproaches at the stranger, he replies with a smile, "Why are you so upset? I can make more of them."

In the tragedies, inequities, and riddles of life, where is God? But we are not the first to ask this question. Neither was Mark Twain. The people of Judah were asking it 2,400 years ago, in the time of the Prophet Malachi. Like Twain, they seemed to have lost God. Where were those glorious, saving deeds of the past? What was the explanation for their present poverty and oppressions? Didn't it pay to serve God?

And when we move from asking where God is in a given situation and ask whether it pays to serve God, the next question is this: Is it worthwhile to continue to believe and practice those features of our faith which distinguish us from our neighbors? After all, to be different is to invite pain and loneliness. Are the rewards of serving God worth that cost?

This is exactly what the Judeans wanted to know. Unable to find God in their daily lives, they had given up. Why try to work up an experience that wasn't there? Why try to maintain distinctives from their neighbors, when it all seemed so empty anyway? As a result, they were well on their way to being absorbed into the generalized paganism of the day.

Such absorption was happening all around them. When the Persian Empire brought together many formerly separate cultures and religions, it became obvious that there was a lot of common ground among the various religions. While the chief god might be called Zeus in one religion and Nabu or Baal in another, he was really the same god underneath, wasn't he? The Jews were bowing to the pressure more and more often. "They call him Baal; we call him Yahweh; so what's the difference?"

Of course, they didn't expect to lose their faith or turn their backs on God. And neither do we, when we succumb to cultural pressures. It's just that we no longer feel it necessary to serve Him as carefully as we once did. We can relax and "enjoy life" a little more.

Unfortunately, that careless life is like a garden in which the gardener has stopped his meticulous cultivating. Precisely because the soil has been tended and well-prepared, the growth of weeds is positively luxuriant. Then one day we may find that our faith is simply not there anymore. Or if it is, it is only a spindly, anemic-looking petunia among the weeds.

Such an outcome was a real possibility for the Judeans. And if it did happen, what then? Was all of God's patient self-revelation across the centuries going to be lost? Even more important, what of all the preparation for the perfect revelation of the Messiah? If the people of God simply accommodated themselves to a genial and meaningless paganism, the whole foundation for the coming of the Messiah would be eroded and gone in a matter of years. What of those centuries of patient training? What of "the fullness of time" into which Christ was to come? The stakes were very high.

They are equally high today. Some historians have called this the post-Christian age. Whether or not that is a true judgment, it certainly *is* true that Christian values and understandings of life are no longer automatically learned in America.

Those values and understandings will be preserved and proclaimed only as you and I find such a vitality and reality in our faith that we will dare to be different, even if being different is unpleasant, difficult, or expensive. The Muslims did not need the sword to wipe out 700 years of Christianity in North Africa. All they had to do was levy a tax on Christians which Muslims did not have to pay. Suddenly a lot of people found their Christianity was not nearly as important to them as they had thought.

Divine Presence

Whether such harassment of Christians may come, we cannot say. But if it should, collapse of faith need not follow. We can find a sense of God's reality and presence that will enable us to stand up to all pressures to conform. This is what happened in Judea. There were men and women equal to the challenge. Through them God was able to convince the Judean people

● that He was there.

● that He could be depended on.

● that it was worth the effort to keep the faith, even if their effort marked them as peculiar people. Although some of the Jews went serenely on their way, enough others caught hold of God—or let God get hold of them—in such a way that their lives were changed. No more of the mediocre for them! They would be wholly His.

The sophisticated Romans and Greeks looked at the Jews with both amusement and exasperation. "Why get worked up about religion, for heaven's sake?" We may expect the same kinds of reactions from our neighbors today. But something happened to the people of Judah in their crisis moment. Something which kept them from drifting quietly off into oblivion. Something which made their faith the vehicle through which the tired paganism of Greece and Rome could be put to rest and replaced with a triumphant Christianity.

A faith like that can be ours today. One of the people God used to capture the mind and heart of Judah was a prophet named Malachi. The message of God which made the difference for Judah is recorded in the Book of Malachi.

Because I am convinced that God is saying some things through Malachi which are directly relevant to our lives today, I have written this book. If you and I can get hold of God's message to Malachi, we will discover what we need for today. We will see the real problem and God's solution. We will know the heart of God and our own hearts. And we will learn how we may come to that joyous confidence of His presence which makes life worth living.

Where are You, God? We believe You are here! And we set out with joyous hearts to trace Your footsteps and hear Your voice. Help us to live this day, not with all our questions answered, but with a consciousness of Your reality and a confidence in Your goodness which will shape all the rest of our lives.

2
HOW DO YOU
LOSE GOD?

How do you lose God? Losing God is like losing the Empire State Building, and yet it happens so easily. An agnostic scientist was asked what destroyed his childhood faith. He replied, "It wasn't destroyed. I just put it in a drawer on the day I started my studies. Years later when I needed my faith, I opened the drawer to get it. But the drawer was empty."

Lose God? Yes, lose the sense of His importance and reality for your life. Deny Him? Become an atheist? No, just live as if He didn't exist! Polls taken in the United States consistently show that 90 to 95 percent of us believe in the existence of some Supreme Being or Force which could be identified as God. Yet, it is obvious that God and His will are of little importance in the daily lives of most people, including Christians.

How about you? If you were to rank the importance of God in your daily life, what would you say? Is He very important, fairly important, or rather unimportant? Because you're reading this book, my guess is that He is pretty important to you, or that you would like Him to be. But what has happened to others could happen to you. Without ever intending it, the people of Judah simply lost the sense that God mattered very much.

In this chapter we are going to look at the path which brought the Judean people to this low point in their experience with God. As we do, we are going to see the steps which any nation or people follows as it loses God.

There are really two phases in the story of Judah's tragedy. The first extends from the death of King Solomon in 931 B.C. to the destruction of Jerusalem in 586 B.C. The second phase extends from that destruction until the time of Malachi in about 430 B.C. Although the political conditions during the two periods were very different, the basic problems in the people's relation to God were much the same.

First Phase

In 950 B.C. the nation of Israel was one of the most powerful nations in the Near East. Solomon had developed his father's empire into a kingdom whose wealth and power were a source of wonder to the surrounding nations. There seemed to be no limits to what Israel could do and become under God's blessing.

Yet, within 25 years the empire was lost, the nation split in two, and God's prophets were beginning to speak of coming destruction. It took 350 years before the final aspects of that destruction took place; yet the prophets could see the seeds germinating only a few years after Solomon's death. What happened?

Paganism was what happened, and Solomon himself was partly responsible. When he married the daughters of foreign kings, Solomon followed the custom of the day in allowing them to bring their idols to Jerusalem and build chapels for them on the outskirts of the city. How easy it must have been for the people to justify their own idolatry, since the king himself permitted his wives to practice it.

When Solomon died and Jeroboam led the 10 northern tribes in a revolt against Solomon's son Rehoboam, it must have seemed quite natural for Jeroboam to set up images of bulls in the new worship centers at Bethel and Dan. It is almost certain that he did not think of himself as departing from the faith. He probably only wanted to make Yahweh more visible—and more attractive, so that worshipers would not want to go to Jerusalem, capital of the enemy state, Judah.

But whatever Jeroboam's motives, the prophets saw what the eventual outcome of his actions would be. To represent God with images was to leave the faith of the fathers and to become pagans.

How does this departure of Israel and Judah relate to our situation?

We are not about to make an image of God. In fact, to most of us a fat, brooding Buddha or a jewel-encrusted Vishnu is rather repulsive. So how do we have anything in common with the Hebrews and their idol worship?

Idols are only a symptom of a deeper problem and it is quite possible to have the problem without manifesting this particular symptom. But what is the problem? An understanding of life and of the world which is directly contrary to that found in the Bible. The prophets recognized that the idolatry of Israel and Judah were symptomatic of this disease, and they attacked the symptoms in order to destroy the disease. Just because we do not manifest the symptom of idols, we dare not immediately conclude that we do not have the disease. A disease can be all the more dangerous when its normal evidences are obscured. And its victim might be very far gone before the disease is detected.

In much of the Western world today, we do not represent the gods with images, but we look at the world in much the same way as does an idolator. Let me show you what I mean.

First of all, let's go back to Israel and Judah and try to understand what their idolatry said about their understanding of life. Then we will be in a position to see where we are tempted to understand the world in the same way, even if we don't yet manifest the same symptoms that they did.

To make an image of a god is to try to express that god in the forms of the visible world—animal, human, or inanimate object. Why would a person want to do that? One reason might be to make deity more understandable. To think of a god who is completely other than we are is not only frightening but frustrating. How do you relate to a god like that? But if you can put that being into the forms of this world, it becomes understandable. Even more, it becomes *biddable*, an old word meaning "capable of being asked for things."

This last idea takes us close to what idolatry is all about. For the idolator, though it is interesting to know *about* the gods, it is not really necessary. What *is* necessary is knowing how to get the gods to do what you want. If the forces which shape your destiny, which determine whether you succeed or fail, are really not tied into the visible, sensory world, how can you influence them? The idolater puts the gods into some form in which he can influence their actions in his favor.

For instance, you have some idea of how to relate to powerful humans—flattery, cajolery, adulation, gifts, or threats. Now if you understand the deities as superhumans, you can use the same approaches on them.

What does it mean to say that the gods are like us, but merely on a larger scale? It means that the gods had a beginning like we did and, conceivably, an end like we shall have. It means that just as sex is fundamental to our existence, so it is to theirs. Just as we are ethically undependable, so are they.

According to this understanding, all that *is* exists within the realm of human experience—physically, socially, and psychologically. Nothing exists outside that realm. There are no absolute ethical principles to be imposed from outside. There is no *outside*. Furthermore, everything *inside* is tightly connected. If you manipulate the system in a certain way, you get a desired effect.

In practice, this means

● that I can manipulate the gods—those forces which shape human destiny—or at least align myself with them, through manipulation of the physical, psychological, and social systems.

● that the only consistency in the universe is mindless and mechanical.

● that ethically consistent behavior is of no use in the achievement of security.

● that there is no security for me except that which I get for myself.

How does all this apply to us? We would agree that an idolator views the world in a nonbiblical manner. But not only idolators hold that position. The previous paragraphs present the world view of many modern Westerners. They have made the gods to be faceless forces which they approach in the same idolatrous attitudes as the ancients did their gods.

What did this slide toward idolatry mean for the Judeans and the Israelites? It meant they began to see God as existing primarily for them. Their purposes and their security were paramount. The next step was to believe that through correct performance of rituals, they could insure that God would grant them security.

This led to the conviction that consistent ethical behavior was not really necessary, if the rituals were performed properly. The prophets of God recognized all this as nearly complete perversion of the truth which God had been revealing.

Far from God existing for humans, the opposite is true. We exist for Him. He is not part of the observable universe and cannot be manipulated through it. God is consistent in His purposes and behavior. His settled plan is to bless His people and make them secure in every way, but that security is realizable only when they abandon their self-centered attempts to gain that security, and instead, commit themselves to Him to live according to His plans.

We often have difficulty understanding the prophets. When we like what they're saying, we see them as popular preachers in the modern-day mold. When their words convict us, we see them as crusty curmudgeons who wouldn't know a good time if it fell on them.

The prophets were men and women who had fallen in love with God and had glimpsed the glory of His character, the purity of His truth, and the wonder of His dreams for humanity. It is not surprising that they were horrified when they discovered that their compatriots had "exchanged the truth about God for a lie, and worshiped and served the creature rather than the Creator, who is blessed forever!" (Rom. 1:25)

The prophets saw all too clearly that it was a commitment to self which led

● to craven and corrupt leadership.
● to alienation between rich and poor.
● to ritual which sought control rather than worship.
● to manipulation of persons rather than commitment to them.
● to an attempt to appropriate God's power without possessing His character.

For all these reasons, the prophets wept and shouted, denounced, pled, and wooed. Yet the people were amazed that anyone should impute such awful things to them. They were like blind people walking toward a cliff, but claiming that they were strolling in an upland meadow.

The prophets depicted the terrors ahead in vivid colors: The land did not belong to Israel in perpetuity. It was theirs only as long as they obeyed its Master. Now it was about to spew them out. Expecting the Day of the Lord, were they? It would come all right, but be nothing like they expected. The Holy would consume their unholiness, the Straight their twistedness. It would be a day of "darkness and not light; as when a man flees from a lion, and a bear meets him" (Amos 5:18-19, NASB).

Even when the inevitable happened and North Israel was destroyed by Assyria in 721 B.C., the Judeans refused to believe it could happen to them. After all, they had God's temple in Jerusalem and God would never destroy that. A frustrated Jeremiah cried out,

> "Do not trust in deceptive words saying, 'This is the temple of the Lord, the temple of the Lord, the temple of the Lord.' . . . Will you steal, murder, and commit adultery, and swear falsely, and offer sacrifices to Baal, and walk after other gods that you have not known, then come and stand before Me in this house, which is called by My name, and say, 'We are delivered!'—that you may do all these abominations?" (Jer. 7:4, 9-10, NASB)

Carried off to Babylon in 598 B.C., Ezekiel had the same difficulty convincing the other exiles that God really was going to destroy Jerusalem. Or that He preferred holy living to holy places and careful ethics to careful cult. Self-deception had run its full course, as it always will when our security and our plans are allowed to become uppermost.

In 586 B.C. God's righteous judgment fell, as the holy city was breached and burned, and the key leadership taken into captivity in Mesopotamia. It is hard for us to imagine the despair which gripped the Judeans. What they were so certain couldn't happen had happened. Surely the grand experiment was all over. The people of God would be scattered over the earth. If ever God seemed dead, it was on that day. His city was in ruins. His house was desecrated. He had not defended Himself or His people.

Even now on the anniversary of the destruction of the temple—tradition holds that the destruction of both Solomon's and Herod's temples occurred on the same date—synagogues are darkened and no voice is heard.

Second Phase

But it was not all over. When the prophets had announced judgment to come, they had also promised that God would never forsake His people. Although the land had spewn them out, God never would. To be restored to His favor, they had only to repent and believe. But convincing the people there was hope was almost as hard as convincing them they had been in danger.

Ezekiel's second task was as draining as his first. Having foretold the destruction of Jerusalem, he was now called upon to announce the return of the Judeans from exile. But how could that be, when no people had ever returned from exile?

At first the Judeans would not believe it, but slowly they came to understand that as the prophets had been correct in their prediction of destruction, so they might also be correct in their prediction of a restoration. And what a restoration it was to be! Jerusalem would be the center of the world. She would teach God's law; all nations would come humbly to her, and all their wealth would flow into her. It would be a time of peace and reconciliation, for the warring elements of the universe would be put to rest, and harmony and light would prevail. It would be the Age of the Messiah, God's Ruler who would set up His kingdom on the earth. The wisdom, justice, and righteousness for which the world was pining would come to pass.

As the people of Judah pored over their Scriptures, they were finally able to see the whole picture. What fools they had been. God had longed to bless them, would have blessed them, if they had only let Him. And He still meant to do so. Would they let Him? Oh yes! How often prayers of repentance and faith, similar to Daniel's prayer (Daniel 9) must have been offered in those years. And what was the result?

As certainly as the dawn, the restoration came, even though neither the Assyrians nor the Babylonians had ever let anyone return. In God's providence the Persians replaced the Babylonians and the Persian Emperor Cyrus became God's servant. So the first small band of Judeans returned to the rubble of Jerusalem. It had happened! Hope was born. Surely this was just the foretaste of all the rest of the promises being fulfilled. So they waited. And waited.

The second temple was finally finished, after a hiatus of some 16 years between the laying of the foundation and the continuation of the work. Perhaps that hiatus was due to the first pinprick in the balloon of their hopes. Present at the laying of the foundation were some who were old enough to remember the former temple. To them it was obvious that this temple would be smaller than Solomon's. What about all those grandiose dreams? Their weeping and rejoicing were indistinguishable (Ezra 3:13).

As the years passed, the Jews began to wonder about the promises. They had truly repented and believed God. They had committed their lives and their security to Him. Why weren't they the richest nation in the world? Why wasn't Jerusalem the Queen of the Nations, instead of the ruined county seat of a little backwater out on the fringes of the Persian Empire? Where was the Messiah? Where was the Golden Age?

Slowly, almost imperceptibly, they began to lose God, as their forefathers had four centuries earlier. In the well-defined suffering of exile, they had found Him. But now the outlines were becoming hazy.

There would be no idols this time. They had lost their land and gone into exile because they had made idols. They had believed that if idols were never again used, they would never again lose God. But they did. How? They viewed service to God as a way to get what they wanted and needed. And they tried to make Him serve them.

This never has worked—then or now. When our self-centeredness blocks the channels of His grace, God cannot give us what He wants to. Then when we don't get what we want, we conclude it is futile to serve Him. Why break our necks doing what He asks when we don't get anything out of it? So instead, we devote our time to those forces or powers or activities—gods—which do produce. Of course, it could be dangerous to simply neglect Him. But there is no reason to be fanatical about serving Him.

This was the path the Jews took, between the return from Exile and the time of Ezra, Nehemiah, and Malachi. They did not revert to idols, but their understanding of life was idolatrous. As they placed a high premium on rituals and a low premium on faithfulness, they slowly lost touch with God as a vital reality.

The same thing happens in our own time. When we think God

exists to serve us, we have begun to embrace a pagan world view. To manipulate Him, we must remove Him from His transcendant lordship and make Him a part of our finite world. But the more He is shaped according to our desires and goals, the less we are conformed to His radical consistency. When we discover that God is not producing according to our plans, we try to manipulate other forces—gods—to get what we want. All along this dreary way, our commitment to what is right is growing more fuzzy until "what is right" becomes indistinguishable from what we want. In the end God is lost to us.

Is there any cure? Yes! That is what the Book of Malachi is about. God can be found. Franco Zefferelli dramatizes it well in his film version of Francis of Assisi's life. The medieval church reduced God to the status of guarantor of its security, yet continued to allow the transcendant Word to be read in the hearing of the people. Thus, the young Francis was able to hear and be gripped by that Word. Convinced that devotion to God demanded a life of simplicity and goodness, Francis poured out his vision to an obese and venial bishop. While fearing and hating Francis, the bishop had to respond that his vision did seem consistent with Scripture. And as we allow the Scriptures to speak and to judge us, God will cleanse and free us from ourselves.

Oh God, where are You? The fog of our selfishness has closed down upon us. We dare to believe You are there, but somehow You must send a light bright enough to penetrate the fog, and light the way to Yourself.

3
IS GOD REALLY THERE?

The oracle: the word of the Lord to Israel through Malachi.
Malachi 1:1

The destruction of Jerusalem in 586 B.C. had lacerated to rawness the spirits of the people of God. They asked themselves, "What's happening? What have we done? How can we get out of this awful mess?" Then they were painfully, dreadfully awake.

But now, in 430 B.C., they were in a drugged stupor, too lethargic to care. It all seemed so useless anyway. But *now* they were in danger. T.S. Eliot wrote, "This is the way the world ends, not with a bang, but a whimper." In the long history of God's dealings with mankind, few have ever had their faith violently torn from them. Rather, most have just watched it drift away. When they realized it was gone, they felt a vague emptiness, but no real distress. Someone has correctly said, "Loss of faith is rarely a blowout. More commonly it is a slow leak."

But what was God to do for His people? And what is God to do for us? For we are not simply speaking of Judeans in the fifth century B.C. Christians of our own century stand in the same danger.

If Christianity ever dies in North America, it will not be because a jack-booted commissar steals it from us. Rather, it will be that we blithely let go of the realities of our faith as we reach for the lust of the flesh, the lust of they eyes, and the pride of life. Then when we are prodded by some pressure, be it political, social, or ethical, our faith will be revealed as a husk, hardly worth the pain to defend.

Miracles

How could God stop this erosion of faith? How could He demonstrate His reality and His presence? One way would be to perform a miracle, do a sign. Surely that would prove God's presence and power. Or would it? How many miracles does it take, how many signs must there be, to convince a reluctant human will? There will never be enough. Think of the signs and wonders of the Exodus. If ever a generation of people had reason to believe that God was present and active, it was the Children of Israel. Yet are they known for radiant faith? Courageous endeavor? No, but for complaining, grumbling, a resolute unwillingness to trust God. At every turn, they chose death rather than life.

Jesus' generation was blessed with signs and wonders, with undeniable proofs of His divinity. Yet what was the result? The Apostle John tells of the rulers of the Jews asking Jesus for a sign that they might see and believe (John 6:30). But they had just seen the feeding of the 5000! What more could they ask? Like their forefathers, they really did not want to believe.

There is no miracle which can make a rebellious will bow down. How many miracles would it take for Satan and his angels to bow before God? They know He is God. They need no miracles to convince them. Nothing external can make them worship.

Miracles can be counterfeited. If our faith is in the miracles and not in God, we are forced to change brands. The story is told of a teacher in Stalinist Russia who was faced with an unusually devout group of children. She tried several means of talking them out of their childlike faith, but had little success. Finally, she asked the children if they believed in prayer. They responded with a resounding Yes. She asked them to pray to God for candy, reminding them that the Bible promises that if we ask anything in faith, God will give it. So the little heads were innocently bowed in prayer. In a few moments, she asked those who had received candy to raise their hands. No hands were raised and there were some troubled looks. She told them to bow their heads again and this time to ask Comrade Stalin for candy. As they were praying she passed silently down the rows putting a bag of candy on each desk. When the children opened their eyes, the teacher had won. Comrade Stalin was the miracle worker. The other God was a failure.

No, miracles are not the answer. They can support faith already in existence, but they cannot create faith in an atmosphere of distrust and doubt. Moreover, an overdependence on miracles can be a positive detriment to faith, because faith itself is the evidence of things unseen. A trust which rests largely upon things seen will not stand firm in the spiritual battles of life. This is not to say we should not expect miracles of God's power and grace in our lives. We should. But miracles should not be the basis of our faith. For they come in seasons and according to God's sovereign will. He gives them when He chooses and withholds them when He chooses. Either way our faith is in Him.

Malachi as Messenger

But then how can God reveal Himself and His truth in such a way as to catch our attention and help us to understand? The answer is summed up in the name of the Prophet Malachi. His name means "My Messenger." It is so appropriate to the situation and content of his book that some Bible students have thought it was a pen name. While this is possible, God may have providentially guided Malachi's parents in the choice of a name for their child, one which would fit his future work.

Malachi's name expresses God's answer to the problem of human doubt and fear. God sent a personal messenger. Miracles are not sufficient and neither are abstract ideas. This is not to say that ideas are not important, for they are. God in His revelation has disclosed concepts and propositions of an earthshaking nature. To really understand scriptural principles and ideas is to hold a radically different view of the meaning of life than most of the world has. To fail to build these concepts into our lives is to be flabby and flaccid, easy prey for every new fad which flits through our vacant brains.

But ideas, concepts, principles, and propositions are in themselves lifeless. There is nothing in all the world so dead as people who have all the right ideas but no dynamic by which to put those ideas into flight. This is why the Bible is not a list of rules, collection of proverbs, or compendium of philosophical axioms. God chose to show His truth through the lives of people. He embodied ideas in persons.

This is why the Book of Genesis and the Gospels are special favorites of most people. These books in a particular way convey God's truths through people's lives. Most of the Bible is rooted in life situations. God has given us His Word in this way because of our needs as human beings. We are not merely rational, but also physical and emotional. Ideas cannot bleed or weep, laugh or sing, but people can. Therefore, until we see an idea worked out in life, incarnated, we are skeptical of it, and rightly so.

Bishop Addison Hosea, bishop of the Lexington, Kentucky diocese of the Episcopal Church, tells the story of a former parishioner who, when asked why he was not in church on summer Sundays, reported that he and his family went to their cabin on the Kentucky River for weekends and that he was usually fishing on Sunday mornings. "But," he added piously, "I'm with you in spirit, Father." The Bishop looked him squarely in the eye and said, "Buddy, next week you get your carcass in the third row on the aisle, where you usually sit, and let your *spirit* go fishing!"

As the Bishop so neatly pointed out, our spirits are normally where our bodies are and visa versa. Until an idea has been enfleshed, it has little impact upon us. This explains why God so often dealt with the Old Testament people through angelic messengers. A good case in point is Joshua. He knew rationally that God was the Commander of the armies of Israel. But in reality, Joshua was still carrying the awful responsibility. This became clear when he met the battle-clad angel. With great courage Joshua confronted him to ask, "Are you for us or them? Can I count on you to help me, or must I get rid of you now so I can get on with the job?" What a jolt when the messenger said, "Neither. I came to lead you." The idea of God's leadership had been incarnated and Joshua not only *knew* it, but *saw* and *felt* it. (See Joshua 5:13-15.)

The solution to the doubts and problems facing the Jewish people of Malachi's day were first of all answered in the prophet himself. The people were asking, "God, can You really hear us? Does it really matter what we do? Where are You when we suffer and struggle and it all seems so useless?" God's answer was a person! He could have written "I love you" on the Milky Way. He could have showered them with tightly reasoned tracts from a celestial "Gospel Blimp." He could have caused the thunder to shout, "Yes, I hear you when you cry." Instead, He sent a person, the Prophet Malachi. And today to meet our needs He sends a person to put an arm around our shaking shoulders, to mingle their tears with ours, and not so much give an answer as *be* an answer in themselves.

There is an often-told story about two little girls who sat on a curb, weeping as though their hearts would break. A sensitive passerby stopped and asked the first little girl what was wrong? She sobbed out, "I've lost my dolly."

"Oh, that's too bad," he said. "And what about you?" he asked the other little girl. "Did you lose your dolly too?"

"No," said the little girl. "I just stopped to cry with her." Because you love, I dare to believe God loves. Because you care, I dare to believe God cares. Because you are here, I dare to believe God is here.

The very fact of Malachi's preaching was evidence that God knew their needs. To be sure, what he had to say was not all pleasant. Yet, if God was to do what they cried for, if He was to demonstrate His love and power to them, He must, like a surgeon, first cut in order to heal. And the message which came to Malachi was a burden. It settled down as a weight, a pressure which would grow until released.

Being God's person in a given situation may not win us acclaim, appreciation, or even respect. We do young people a disservice when we encourage them to live uncompromisingly for Christ "because people will respect you." Probably most will ignore us or dismiss us contemptuously. Some may even actively hate us.

This was the experience of John Wesley, a man of massive intellect, unimpeachable integrity, and a gentle concern for people. Yet his detractors tried to outdo each other in applying vile names to him, calling him everything from "ignorant infidel" to "clever charlatan." Yet he went steadily and quietly on his way, reaching tens of thousands for Christ. Why did he do it? Because the burden of the

Lord was upon him and he intended to be faithful to that call. Such obedience bears its own message: If God's messenger is faithful, whether applauded or derided, then I can believe his God is just as faithful.

Yet this burden, this call to be the messenger of God, is not like other burdens. The words of Jesus come to mind: "My yoke is easy, and My burden is light" (Matt. 11:30, KJV). Viewed by themselves those phrases seem contradictory: by definition, a yoke is hard and a burden is heavy.

When Jesus' statements are seen in the context of the Near East, we begin to understand. The great tyrants of the ancient world delighted to boast how they had subdued this nation and that, how they had broken their wills and crushed their spirits. They loved to announce, "We put our heavy yoke upon them." Now we see what Jesus meant. Yes, there is a surrender we must make, there is an obedience we must render. But it is not to some arrogant monster who wishes to devour us as food for his own ego. Rather, it is the surrender of the loved one to the lover. It is the opening of my small treasure to the One who wishes to put each gem in gorgeous settings to display to the world.

And why should the burden of being God's messenger be light? Because He who lays it upon us also carries it with us. But so often we do not avail ourselves of this truth. We are like the man who was staggering along the road carrying a heavy load on his back. A wagon driver, seeing his difficulty, stopped and offered him a ride. Gratefully, the man climbed up and settled himself on the box with a sigh. But he still had his load on his back. The driver looked at him in surprise. "Why don't you throw that in the back of the wagon?" he asked. "Oh," replied the passenger, "you're already carrying me. I couldn't ask you to carry my pack too." Foolish, we say. Yet, how often each of us staggers along under some burden Christ has asked us to assume, never realizing that He already bears us *and* the burden. We may execute the task faithfully, yet without being crushed by it. The burden *is* light.

Messiah as Messenger

So far we have talked only about Malachi's messengership as being the fulfillment of his name and a partial answer to the questions the

Judeans were proposing. But there is more to it than that. Malachi called the priests the messengers of the Lord of hosts and said they were condemned because of their failure to embody God's nature in their lives and teachings (Mal. 2). Judah had lost her sense of God's presence and reality because these men failed.

But Malachi mentioned another messenger, in chapter 3. In fact, in the light of Malachi 4:5, *two* other messengers are being spoken of in chapter 3. Since more will be said about these later, we will not go into detail here. But it is important to see how those references fit into the theme of this chapter.

God's answers to the genuinely vexing questions concerning His justice in the world are not found in philosophy books. They are found in caring, faithful persons who have met Him and love Him and therefore love others. How do we know this is His way? Because of His Son! God Himself has done the thing He calls us to do. He has embodied all of His truth in a Person.

Malachi 2 closes on an angry, lonely note as the people of Judea indict God for not destroying evil people and blessing good people on a day-by-day, tit-for-tat basis. What is God's answer? How does He confront the problems of evil and justice in the world? "Behold, I will send My Messenger" (3:1). And who was the Messenger but His Son!

God does not stand off and judge sin and evil and tragedy from a distance. No, He bears it, He takes it upon Himself. There is justice. Where is God? He is with us—Immanuel.

God's love and mercy and the eventual triumph of righteousness also needed to be incarnated. God could tell of His mercy and holiness, but the reaction of a weary world would only be, "That's nice. What else is new?" The reality that the One who made all things is love simply does not touch us until we see Jesus putting flesh on that love and dying for us. And when He bursts from the tomb, shattering the evil which shut Him there, then we *know* evil will not prevail.

The Reverend Walter Albritton tells how as a young seminary student, he had very bitter feelings toward a certain professor who taught some things Walter did not think were scriptural. But when the Albrittons' small son was stricken with leukemia, it was this man who was in the forefront, expressing his love and continuing concern for them all. He visited with them and sat on the floor to play with desperately ill David. He did not try to answer their unspoken questions. It was enough that he was there. Other friends tried to cover their feelings of inadequacy with pious little statements such as, "Perhaps God needs another little cherub in the angel choir." Walter says candidly, "I thought I would hate a God like that."

The day came when, in the wee hours of the morning, David's life ebbed away. In the graying dawn Walter and his wife were sitting listlessly at the kitchen table looking at nothing. There was a knock at the door. When Walter opened it, there stood his professor.

He had heard the news and asked if he might come in. He sat at the kitchen table and shared with them, not so much his answers as his own struggles through a situation of this sort. One thing he said lodged in their hearts. "While we do not know why this happened, we do know this: God is hurting over David's death as deeply as you are." Walter says, "I could love a God like that."

There is God's call to us: to *be* His message. This is not to say that a good life is justification for bad theology. On the other hand, pristine pure theology which has never been enfleshed is a denial of the truth of Jesus Christ. "And the Word was made flesh, and dwelt among us, and we beheld His glory, the glory as of the only begotten of the Father, full of grace and truth" (John 1:14, KJV). God has not answered all our questions; nor can He, given our limitations. But this He has done—He has come to be one with us, to *bear* our griefs and sorrows. And when we cry out in the darkness, "Where are You?" to throw His arm about us and say, "Here."

But sometimes we cannot feel that arm and hear that voice, even when a faithful human brother or sister becomes the messenger. Something prevents us from knowing the comfort of His presence or the reality of His power. This was the position of the Judeans. The whole routine had become so pointless and empty.

O God, we want to feel Your presence. We want to know You're with us. We even want to be Your messenger to someone else. But sometimes You seem so far away. Why, God?

II
THE USE
OF GOD

4
HOW DO YOU KNOW
HIS LOVE?

"I have loved you," says the Lord.
"But you ask, 'How have You loved us?'
"Was not Esau Jacob's brother?" the Lord says.
"Yet I have loved Jacob, but Esau I have hated, and I have
turned his mountains into a wasteland and left his inheritance
to the desert jackals."
Edom may say, "Though we have been crushed,
we will rebuild the ruins."
But this is what the Lord Almighty says: "They may build,
but I will demolish. They will be called The Wicked Land, a
people always under the wrath of the Lord. You will see it
with your own eyes and say, 'Great is the Lord—even beyond
the borders of Israel!'" Malachi 1:2-5.

What does God say to you, when you have allowed the fog of your
own search for security to blot Him out of your sight? How does He
feel about you when your real reaction to His truth is discouragement
and cynicism? What does He say when you succumb to the temptation
to give up on God?

The Judeans had given up on God. This is apparent in their
questions. Whenever God made a statement, their reaction was not
acceptance and faith but disbelief and doubt. "Oh yeah? How?" Nine
times this kind of insolent question was thrown back in God's face, in
Malachi 1:2, 6-7; 2:14, 17; 3:7-8, 13-14. Their predisposition was

not to believe Him, but to question Him.

This is not to say that questions are off limits for believers. By no means. God invites us to test Him, and testing involves examining and questioning. But there are two very different types of testing. One example might be the biblical teaching concerning Creation. The believer says, "Yes, Father, I believe You created this world. Please show me the evidence." The unbeliever says, "God created the world? You're going to have to prove that to me." It will be very hard to convince the second person because there is really no middle ground between belief and disbelief; he is beginning from a position of denial. That was the position to which the Jews of Malachi's day had come.

Now what would God say to them, as He perceived their desperate situation? Surely He would berate them for their sins, and even more for their bad attitude. Surely He would warn them that His patience was wearing thin, and challenge them to shape up *now*! But no. His first word to them, and to you and me was, "I love you."

What? Why would He say this? Doesn't He know you can be too soft? Doesn't He know that people will take advantage of you unless you clamp down hard at the beginning? Why would this be His first word? It surely doesn't sound like the Old Testament God of wrath. Perhaps it is precisely because of this false understanding of Him that He begins in this way.

Who is God? He's the judge in a black robe seated behind a great dark desk on which lies a huge ledger with heavy covers and metal clasps. His satisfaction comes from putting black marks beside our names in that ledger. Day after day, He peers over the edge of heaven, watching. "There goes Simeon, headed right for the ditch. That's just like him. If I've told him once, I've told him a thousand times, 'Stay out of the ditch!' Whoops, there he went. Right in, head first. Well, too bad. That's another black mark for him."

Too many of us think God is out to get us. Oh, we know better with our minds, but our feelings and reactions often go in a "God equals guilt" direction. This is how the Jews of 440 B.C. must have felt. Who is God? "Well, He's the One who punishes us. He has His eye on us to see whether we break the law."

This picture of God as a grim, celestial judge negatively affects our response to Him. If we serve Him only to avoid punishment and guilt, and if we have serious doubts about how much punishment and guilt we are going to be able to avoid anyway, we will serve Him at the lowest possible level.

God did not say to the Judeans, "If you keep that up, I'm going to get you." They already thought God was out to get them. That was part of the reason they were serving Him so poorly. Instead, He spoke those priceless words, "I love you."

Feeling Loved

The motive of avoidance becomes weaker and weaker as it nears its goal. It asks, "How little can I do to escape?" But the motive of attraction becomes stronger and stronger as it nears its goal. It asks, "How much can I do for One who would go to those limits for me?" If we can really be convinced that God does love us, we will do anything for Him. If we are certain of His confidence in us, we can dare to attempt great things for Him, knowing that failure will not change His attitude toward us.

There is no lovelier expression of this love than in the Song of Solomon. There the lover describes the tremendous attraction of his beloved. He compares her to a walled garden from which issue the most delicious scents. The beloved replies by calling on all the winds to come and blow the scents to the lover. "Let my beloved come into his garden and eat its more precious fruits" (Song 4:16, Author's translation). If I can ever believe that God really finds poor, plain me gorgeous and alluring, on that day I will throw open every door and window of my life and shout, "Come into my garden."

In a much more homely vein, the story is told of a little boy in a one-room country school. Because he was very poor, he rarely had a lunch. As a result, he began to steal lunches from other children. The teacher finally caught him red-handed. He called little Jimmy up to the desk to receive the paddling which had been promised to the culprit. As the skinny little fellow bent over the desk and the teacher raised the hefty board, a tall eighth-grader stood up in the back of the room and cried, "Stop!" The teacher looked up, wondering if he had an insurrection on his hands.

"Well, Joseph, what do you want?" The boy, nearly 16 because of months out of school each year helping on the farm, strode down the aisle. At six feet tall he towered over both the teacher and the little culprit.

"Do it to me, Sir," he said. The teacher's eyes widened in surprise, but taking the boy at his word, he motioned Jimmy aside saying, "Watch this carefully, James. This is for you." The teacher put all his weight into the strokes. Barely a groan escaped Joseph's lips, but when it was over and he stood up, his eyes were brimming. Seeing his eyes, Jimmy suddenly burst into a gale of sobs. Throwing his arms around Joe's thighs, he sobbed out. "Joe, I'll never steal anything again. Honest, I won't. And, Joe, if there's ever anything you want done and I can do it, you'll let me know, won't you?"

If the Judeans could ever *feel* that God loved them, their problem would largely be solved. But they did not feel His love. That is made plain by their response to His affirmation. Far from being overwhelmed by His love for them despite their disobedience and apathy, they responded with the first of their cynical questions, "Oh, really? How have You loved us?" One can almost hear the frustrated dreams surfacing. "You love us? Well then, where are the promises? If You love us, why are we still a little backwater? Why are the Persians in control of the world? You love us? Prove it!"

Why is it so hard for us to feel God's love? We can hear this wondrous truth again and again, give vigorous mental assent to it, and yet go on living as though we were slaves, not sons. I think the answer lies in the fact that we have not surrendered to His love.

Have you ever had someone tell you he loves you, when you did not feel the same toward him? Did you *feel* loved? No. You did not doubt his word, and it may have been a rather ego-satisfying experience, but you did not feel loved. Oh, you could take what he had to offer, and maybe you did. Maybe you even asked him to prove his love—something you never would have asked if you had felt precious and loved. You were using the person for yourself, but had never surrendered yourself.

But how different the day when that special someone said, "I love you." Your spirit and maybe your body as well did handsprings and cartwheels. You were loved! You were loved! Your dear one had picked you out of all the world to love. You were somebody!

What's the difference? Only this: in the second case, you surrendered yourself to be loved. This is so hard to do. We want to use God's love for ourselves, to satisfy our demands. But the law of love never works in that way. Only he who *surrenders* to be loved will *feel* the reality of love.

But how do you make such a surrender? Well, in the first place, you let the lover show love in his or her way, not yours. It is not love which says, like some hot-blooded young boy in the backseat of a car, "If you love me, prove it *this* way." We surrender to be loved by God when we allow Him to love us in His way.

This is exactly what the Judeans would not do. They wanted God to prove His love by fulfilling the ancient promises, *now*. They wanted Him to drive out the Persians, reinstitute the Davidic Kingdom, and make them the rulers of the world, *now*. When God refused to do so, they were sure He did not love them.

What was their problem? They were trying to dictate the demonstration of God's love. Not receiving the desired evidence, they assumed there was no love. Of course there was, but not where they wanted to look. God through His prophet said, "If you want proof of My love for you, compare yourself with Edom. See what hope there is for you and what hopelessness for them and you will know My love." But the Judeans wanted their evidence, not God's.

The same is true for us. If we dictate the evidence or where it will be shown, we may very well conclude, "God doesn't love me." It is not that God will necessarily refuse to meet us on our terms. Rather, that the arrogance which led us to dictate the terms in the first place will probably blind us to the genuine movements of His grace. But if we will open ourselves up to look at His direction, the evidence of His love and care for us will almost jump out, and sometimes from the oddest places.

Have you ever lost a small object on a variegated rug and spent frustrated minutes looking for it, only to have it catch your eye from some distant spot, the moment you sat back with a sigh of defeat? That's how it is with God's love. It is waiting to fall on you the moment you are in a position to receive it. The moment your hands are thrown open in an admission of helplessness, then God can fill those hands with the evidence of His deep and total love for you.

For those of us living in the Christian era, the evidence of God's love is all the more overwhelming. For He did not promise to die for us if we got out of the pigpen and cleaned up. No, while we were still sitting there, anointing ourselves with what we thought was the world's finest cosmetic, a mixture of mud and manure, and with every likelihood we would spit in His eye for His sacrifice, He died for us. That's love!

So God said to the Judeans through His messenger, "Look what has happened to Edom and see by comparison how much I have loved you." The territory of Edom was south of Judah and eastward around the southern end of the Dead Sea. The Edomites and the Israelites had long been rivals, for Jacob was father of the Israelites, and Esau was the father of the Edomites (Gen. 36:16-17). The national aspect of the hatred went back as far as Israel's return from Egypt when the Edomites rudely refused Israel's request to pass through Edom on their way to Canaan and then attacked them as they went around (Num. 20:14-21). The problem only grew worse with the passing years. The Edomites sought to block every gain of Israel. The climax came when the Edomites helped the Babylonians to sack and destroy Jerusalem (Ps. 137:7; Obad. 10-14).

But now Edom's turn had come. Arabs from the desert, a people we know as Nabateans, were steadily moving in and displacing the Edomites who would never again rule their own homeland. In contrast, the Judeans were home again. They had a measure of freedom and could flourish if they would. In comparison with Edom, Judah had received great love from God, if she would only accept the evidence.

Being Rejected

But the statement of God's love has another side, one that is chilling and troubling. We read, "I have loved Jacob, but I have hated Esau." But if God *is* love, how can He hate anybody? And if we go further we see that God is angry *forever* at the Edomites. What's going on here? Does God love some people and eternally hate others?

● There are several important factors to observe. First, whatever this statement means, it must be understood in the light of unequivocal biblical statements of God's universal love. Perhaps the most famous of all is John 3:16, "God so loved . . . that whosoever believes." But also important is Matthew 18:14, "It is not the will of your Father who is in heaven that one of these little ones perish." Alongside these are Paul's words to Timothy: "God our Saviour who desires *all* men to be saved," and "Christ Jesus, who gave Himself as a ransom for *all*" (1 Tim. 2:3-6, NASB). God in His love chooses to save everyone. But He has made His choosing dependent on ours.

Granting this, then what is God saying in this strong phrase? We must come to terms with Mediterranean (and Semitic) speech patterns. Northern Europeans are conditioned to keep their emotions under strict control and seldom say one word more than they mean or feel—and usually many words less than they feel! In the community where I grew up, the thought of a husband and wife shouting at each other was simply unheard-of. Equally unheard-of was any public show of affection.

This extreme reticence is illustrated in the story of the old Vermonter whose wife had gone into decline. When the pastor visited her and inquired as to what was wrong, she said she just felt so unappreciated. In 40 years of marriage her husband had only once said, "I love you" and that was on their wedding night. When next he saw the husband, the pastor decided to "take the bull by the horns" and plunge right in. "Mr. MacDonald," he said, "I'm sure your wife would appreciate being told she's loved. Have you done that recently?" The farmer pushed his hat to the back of his head and said, "Waall, Preacher, I don't see why I should. I told Mirandy 40 years ago I loved her and my feelings ain't changed since."

The people of the Mediterranean world are not like that. They are likely to say much more than they feel. Their language is emotional and vital. Observe a couple from Italy or the south of France shouting at each other and then later, equally tumultuously, making up. If I were ever to shout at my wife with that ferocity, we would be living off the emotional aftershocks for weeks. Not so in the case of the people of Malachi's day. They understood that much more was being said than was literally meant. This is called *hyperbole* and is characteristic of the speech of the region.

A good example of hyperbole is found in a New Testament passage which has troubled many people. Jesus said that if a person did not hate his father and mother, and wife and children, he could not serve Him. (See Luke 14:26.) Now does Jesus really mean that you and I should hate our parents? If so, how do we square that with the commandment, "Honor your father and your mother" (Ex. 20:12)? In fact, how do we square it with Jesus' teaching on this commandment when He castigated the Pharisees for creating a loophole in their tradition so that they no longer were required to care for their aged parents (Mark 7:11)? The point is this: if we come to the place where our loyalty to our parents conflicts with our loyalty to Christ, He must come first. Unless my love for Christ is so strong that by comparison my continuing love for my parents looks like hate, then I have not truly committed myself to Christ. I continue to bear a responsiblity to love and honor, and if necessary, care for my parents; but my commitment to Christ is on a completely higher plane.

This gives a partial explanation of God's saying concerning Esau. When you compare how God has treated Israel to how He has treated Edom, His treatment of Edom looks like hate. He is speaking hyperbolically.

● But a second factor also enters in here. In the Hebrew, neither *love* nor *hate* are primarily emotional words. They reflect acts of the will. Thus to love is to choose, while to hate is to reject. This also sheds light upon Christ's statement. To "love" Christ and "hate" our parents is to choose to obey Christ over all other earthly claims, whenever those claims conflict with His claims. It is not to feel emotional revulsion toward our parents.

Likewise, God is saying that He rejected Edom. Why? Is it because He made a primordial decision to reject Esau and all his descendants? The scriptural account gives no reason to think so. To be sure, Jacob was chosen for a place of higher honor, but this did not mean Esau could never experience God's favor and blessing. There is no evidence in the Old Testament that God entertained hatred for or rejected the person Esau. As a matter of fact, Esau is presented in the Genesis account as the injured party, and is shown to have possessed a remarkable degree of grace, for he did freely forgive Jacob.

Rejection by God is always based on negative moral response. Remember the story of Cain and Abel? God said to Cain, "If you do well, will not your countenance be lifted up? And if you do not do well, sin is crouching at the door; and its desire is for you, but you must master it" (Gen. 4:7, NASB). Obedience means acceptance; disobedience means rejection. Esau's descendants, the nation of Edom, were rejected not because of some divine choice made before their father's birth, but because of their continuing rejection of God.

In the same way the descendants of Jacob, the Judeans, were not accepted because Jacob had been chosen before birth, but because they obeyed through repentance and belief. Both before and after the Exile, the prophets called for Israel to turn from her wicked ways and be healed. The remnants of the 10 northern tribes refused and were never brought back. But certain of the Judeans did repent (Daniel 9). This is not saying that repentance and faith *earn* God's love, for it is given freely to everyone. But you cannot receive and enjoy His love unless you repent and believe.

● If you block God's love, as the Edomites did, you put yourself in a dangerous position. This is a third aspect of this word *hate*. The same thing which can bless you can also kill you. It depends on your relationship to that thing.

Electricity is like that. Years ago *Life* magazine showed pictures of an experiment. A man standing on a carefully insulated metal globe was holding a wire which was charged with 13,000 volts of electricity. His hair stood on end and he reported that he felt "tingly." It was what you might call an electrifying experience. However, because he was not grounded the electricity did not actually travel through him, and he was unharmed. On the other hand, had he stepped off that globe onto the ground, he would have been killed instantly. Why? Because the electricity "liked" him one way and "disliked" him the other? No. His own condition determined the impact of the electric charge. The nature of the electricity did not change.

So it is with God's love. To accept it, to live in it, is an exhilarating, life-changing experience. To refuse that power which is reaching out to redeem the world, to ground it, is to destroy yourself.

Believing God

To change the image, God's love is like a blast furnace. Thus Isaiah says, "Who among us can live with continual burning?" (Isa.

33:14, NASB) And the writer to the Hebrews says, "Our God is a consuming fire" (Heb. 12:29, NASB). Nevertheless, to repent and believe is to be enabled to revel in its blaze for now and eternity, and like the three Hebrews of Daniel's day, not even to have the smell of smoke upon us, because we walk with the Son. (See Daniel 3.) But to attempt to stand before its fiery breath in our own strength and merit is to be ruined.

Yet how easily we humans do that. The folly of it! Most people believe in a divine being, but how few of us care to think that perhaps the meaning of our lives is being judged by the standard of His character and purposes. We simply do not follow out the logical implications of our belief. Either He is or He is not the all-powerful originator and His will all-pervasive. Nevertheless, like the Edomites we say, "We are shattered, but *we* will rebuild." *Who* will rebuild? Not we, as long as we are running counter to the love which made and sustains the universe.

The prophets had a favorite title to express this all-powerful, all-pervasive God who confronts us—"the Lord of hosts." Literally, it means "the Lord of armies," but these armies are the heavenly hosts who do whatever God asks.

The concept is of One who has unlimited resources at His control. He has only to speak a word, and host upon host march forth to carry it out. In our arrogance or fear or just plain blindness, too many of us forget this. Elisha's servant Gehazi represents us well. The king of Syria, Ben-Hadad, heard that Elisha was disclosing his secret plans to the king of Israel, so he decided to capture Elisha. Speaking of blindness! If Elisha knew Ben-Hadad's secret plans, then he knew Ben-Hadad was coming to capture him! One morning Gehazi got up and went out on the flat roof of the house where they were staying. He was probably stretching and yawning and rubbing his eyes when suddenly he did a double take. Their village was surrounded by Syrians. He ran back to Elisha's chamber, moaning and groaning and wringing his hands. "Oh what are we going to do? All is lost! We're done for! There's no hope!" I can just see the strained patience with which Elisha looked up and prayed, "Father, open his eyes." As Gehazi stepped out again, he saw what he had not seen before: on all the hills around stood the armies of light. Ben-Hadad thought he had surrounded Elisha, but God had surrounded him. He is the Lord of hosts. (See 2 Kings 6:11-23.)

In a world like ours, how often we say, "Oh, God is so far removed from what's going on here." Not at all. This is precisely why Malachi used this title for God. The Lord of hosts is His Name. He is the God who has all the legions of angels at His hand; the God who is able to work His will in this world. Edom said, "We will rebuild what is shattered." The Lord of hosts replied, "They may rebuild, but I will tear down."

But likewise when His timorous children sigh and say, "What's the use? I just can't do it," the Lord of hosts says, "My child, what you start, I will build, I will bring to completion. I love you. Let Me pick the evidence and then you will see how completely and fully I have loved you."

You don't need to give up on God. In fact, you dare not, for God is an eternal fact of your life. You can't escape Him because He is all about you. That could be a terrifying thought, but it need not be. We can learn not to run from His love, but to run to it and to allow ourselves to be loved. If we can begin to feel that we are loved, our halfhearted efforts in His direction will cease. Instead, we will serve Him from a whole heart, and doing that, we will place ourselves in the stream of His blessing.

Sometimes it's hard for me to feel Your love, God.
I guess I know it with my head, but I just can't feel
I'm really worth it. Show me how to surrender to You,
Lord. Let me stop trying to earn it or make You prove it to
me in my way. Let me just live in it, as in the air I breathe.

5
IS GOD WORTH YOUR BEST?

"A son honors his father, and a servant his master. If I am a father, where is the honor due Me? If I am a master, where is the respect due Me?" says the Lord Almighty. "It is you, O priests, who despise My name.

"But you ask, 'How have we despised Your name?'

"You place defiled food on my altar.

"But you ask, 'How have we defiled You?'

"By saying that the Lord's table is comtemptible. When you bring blind animals for sacrifice, is that not wrong? When you sacrifice crippled or diseased animals, is that not wrong? Try offering them to your governor! Would he be pleased with you? Would he accept you?" says the Lord Almighty.

"Now implore God to be gracious to us. With such offerings from your hands, will He accept you?" says the Lord Almighty.

Malachi 1:6-9

If you are not able to believe that God loves you deeply and genuinely, you may come to despise Him. That's exactly what happened to the Judeans and it also happens today.

In order to understand this, we need to know that the word translated *despise* has a different connotation in Hebrew than in English. For us, *despise* means "to have an extreme emotional revulsion against something or someone." For the Hebrew, it means simply

43

"to consider something or someone worthless." They are not worth time to think about. In some ways the Hebrew idea is more devastating than the English. At least for us, the person is worth getting upset about. For the Hebrew, he's not even worth that.

How much is your God worth? Is He worth your first, your best, or only your castoffs? If you are giving Him only your castoffs, then you do, in fact, despise Him. But why would you put such a low value on Him, the Almighty, the Saviour? Because you don't really believe you can please Him. Because you don't really believe He is on your side. Because you don't really feel that all your efforts for Him are going to get you much further anyhow. He's not worth the trouble.

This is exactly where the people of Malachi's day were. God had asked for a perfect, yearling ram or kid in the various offerings. But they were giving blind, crippled, or sick animals. Why? Because they valued the perfect ones too much to give them to God. They had better uses for them.

All the time they were doing this they were deceiving themselves. Many years before God had designated certain animals as "clean" and others as "unclean." Only clean animals could be offered. Pigs, dogs, and camels, were among the unclean, while sheep, goats, and cattle were clean. A sacrifice was also supposed to be unblemished. The Jews deceived themselves by saying that cleanness was what really mattered, and that if the animal was clean, a few blemishes didn't really matter.

How we love to play with technicalities! The people were insulted when Malachi told them that a blemished animal was the same as an unclean one. For the quality of the sacrifice said something about the heart of the offerer. A heart which would try to palm off a cheap, blemished offering to the Almighty, the Holy One, is an unclean heart.

And we do this when we expect God to be delighted over tarnished trinkets and snippets of time which would leave any earthly ruler outraged. But why are we so careful to please our earthly overlords and yet so careless in what our lives say about the value of the Eternal God?

One reason for such behavior is our inability to believe God loves us. Our relationship to God can be linked to two human relationships:

children to father and servants to master. Although we call God Father and Master, the quality of the relationship does not fulfill what is implied in those terms. We will not correctly value God until these two understandings are worked out in our lives as well as in our words. We must love Him as Father and then fear Him as Master. And both of these must be operative for the proper relationship to exist. If we do not truly love Him, we will do the absolute minimum to get by. If we do not fear Him, we will be tempted to use Him for our own ends.

It may be objected that love which is genuine would never attempt to use its loved one. This is true. But genuine love is built upon an accurate appraisal and appreciation of the loved one. A correct understanding of God must include a reverential awe for His greatness and His majesty which will shape all our actions. That is the fear of the Lord.

Love Him as Father

The highest motivation of all is love. For those we love we will do anything, dare anything. This is why the Book of Malachi begins on that note. If God's people *feel* His love and then respond out of love rather than coercion, the battle is more than half over.

But many of us, like the Judeans, are hindered at that very point. We do not *feel* that God loves us. As a result, we have difficulty responding to Him in love. Why should that be so? Why should God's love be hard to feel?

We have already discussed our reluctance to surrender to His love. But there are two other factors which make it hard for us to receive God's communication.

● Most human beings do not do what they ought to until they are somehow forced into it. In virtually all parts of our society, coercion is the primary motivation for action. The result is that we project this upon God. It is very difficult for us to believe, on an emotional level, that God is not using His love to make us do something.

● The second factor is a conflict between pride and conscience. We want to believe that we have earned, or at least deserve, whatever we possess. Something within us insists upon being able to stand before God and say to Him, "When I have become good enough for Your love, then I'll let You give it to me." It is humiliating to have to admit that someone loves me *in spite of* what I have done and not *because of* it. Yet that is our only hope. For conscience keeps reminding us that we can *never* be good enough to deserve God's love. However pride might delude us, conscience keeps dragging up reality. The result is that whenever the sunlight of God's love would come flooding into the darkened room of our life, conscience slams the door and says, "Sorry, this child's not good enough for that!"

So we go through life pining for the sense of His love. And since we don't have it, we say, "What's the use? I can never measure up to God's standards. I might as well quit trying." This gives conscience more equipment with which to beat us, so we feel less loved and more defeated. As a result we try even less. You get the picture—life becomes an auger, digging itself deeper and deeper into the ground.

How do we reverse the spiral? How do we come up out of that hole and reach for the heights? The prescription is humiliatingly simple, and that's what makes it so hard. Do you remember the story of Naaman, the Syrian general who was afflicted with leprosy? He came to the Hebrew Prophet Elisha for a cure. Surely Elisha would perform some intricate, mysterious ritual which would demand very special instruments and techniques. After all, wasn't he, Naaman, a very special case? How hard it was on his pride to admit that seven simple dives into the insignificant Jordan River would take care of him!

The cure for us is equally simple. When my first child was born, I loved her but not because she was so beautiful. She was red and wrinkled. But my love made her seem beautiful. I didn't love her because she was gifted, but my love made her seem smart.

I never really knew the fatherly love of God until I held my firstborn in my arms. Funny, wrinkled little thing—what was she worth? A few dollars on the chemical market? No. She was worth my life!

Why does God love you? Because you are! Why does God like what you have become? Because He had the major hand in making you the way you are. *You* are God's best gift to you. Don't deprecate His workmanship! He is your Father, the Father you may never have known on earth, the Father whose characteristics your earthly father may have represented well—or poorly. Stop trying to earn His affection; stop seeing a worldly coerciveness in Him. Relax.

Admit to your conscience that in yourself you can never measure up to God's standards, but that God loves you for you, not for your deeds. When conscience slams the door, kick it open again! And let the Son shine in! "God demonstrates His own love for us in this: while we were still sinners, Christ died for us" (Rom. 5:8). "Dear friends, *now* we are the children of God, and what we will be has not yet been made known. But we know that when He appears, we shall be like Him" (1 John 3:2).

Fear Him as Master

But does this mean you can do whatever you like now, secure in the fact of His love? No, not if the other aspect of the relationship is clear, not if you respect Him as your Master. This is what makes His love more wonderful. He doesn't have to love you. He doesn't need you to bolster His ego or stave off His loneliness. In His triune self God is complete. Nor does He need to cajole you into obedience with whining protests of love. One day every knee will bow to Him in heaven and on earth. He is the Master, the Lord.

You need only stand and look at a clear night sky to have this brought home. After you have soaked up that immensity and glory for awhile, then whisper, "And this is only a dim reflection of Thee." I don't know about you, but at that point my knees begin to buckle. He is the Lord. He could do anything He wished with us. He is our Master.

The Jews knew it. Every time they came to His personal name in the Scriptures (probably pronounced Yahweh), they had schooled themselves to say "the Lord" instead. We have retained the practice in our modern Bibles. Whenever THE LORD appears, it is a substitution for God's personal name.

We call Him "Lord" or "Master," yet how easy it is to give the lie to honorific titles. How easy it is to think God exists to serve us, that He is a convenient deity who gives us unending good luck and our opponents all the bad luck. We make Him a senile grandfather in heaven who cannot see through our silly posturings and lofty protestations. Or the "good buddy" on high who lets us know where all life's "smokies" are hiding. We expect to rush into His throne room, give Him a comradely slap on the back, and ask how we can help Him out! Or if He gets in a huff over something, we expect to toss Him a tidbit to butter Him up a bit. We have turned Him into a prayer box to keep under the bed until we need it, then to be whipped out, cranked feverishly for a few minutes, and put back. Who cares whether this kind of God loves us or not? Who cares what His character is, as long as He produces in the pinch?

What I have just described is paganism in biblical dress. And it is just as prevalent today as in Malachi's day. It claims that God exists to serve our ends, and that He will, as we manipulate Him through offerings, vows, and services. "God, I'll give You some presents *if* You bless me."

A long time ago, St. Augustine said, "Idolatry is the use of what should be worshiped and the worship of what should be used." By that definition, God is the idol of all too many who call themselves Christians.

The problem is that when we hold this concept of God, He can't bless us. Oh, we may have more than average income and a relatively untroubled life, and we may attribute these to keeping God on our side. But excitement and joy and serenity and fullness are missing. Our lives are empty and boring. Of our religious life, we say with the Judeans, "What a burden!" Of course. It's like putting on our swimsuit and, clutching inner tubes around our waists, going ankle deep in the water, and then wondering, as we stand there shivering, why everybody gets so excited about swimming. We have never really gotten in the stream. We have never gotten out of our depth and learned the wonder of being borne along. We have never let God be God. "Why call ye Me 'Lord, Lord,' and do not the things that I say?" (Luke 6:46, KJV)

What we have been talking about is the fear of the Lord, or the lack of it. In the Old Testament there is no word for religion, because the Hebrews did not have a compartment for their relationship to God. *Life* was relationship to God. But there were two phrases which summed up for them an appropriate and productive relationship with Him. One was "the knowledge of God" which expresses personal acquaintance with Him. The other was "the fear of the Lord." To be rightly related to Him was to know His place and your place, and order your life accordingly.

Balanced Fear

There are two ditches to avoid when we think about this concept. They stand on either side of the truth. On the one hand, the fear of the Lord is not terror. Have you ever talked to a little boy who cringed every time you raised your hand to scratch your ear? Why did he do that? He had been hit so many times from so many directions and for so many different things that he just automatically winced every time an adult hand was raised. That is terror. It is the fear of an arbitrary tyrant who will destroy you at a whim or give you a stomachache if you don't pray before eating a hotdog. Such fear gives sweaty palms and ulcers, and reduces you to a wreck in the face of a decision.

That is not the fear of the Lord. "The fear of the Lord is clean, enduring forever" (Ps. 19:9, KJV). The God whom we know is not an arbitrary tyrant. To be sure, His ways are above our ways: who can sort out all the implications of divine sovereignty and human freedom? But He is consistent in all that we know of Him. He does not one day order us to steal and the next day hit us for stealing. He does not condemn His followers for some excess and then indulge in it Himself. He is consistent and He may be known. And in knowing Him we can also know what is right and wrong, and how we will be judged.

On the other side, the fear of the Lord is much more than *respect*, as that word is used today. For instance, Abraham explained to the Philistine King Abimelech that he lied about Sarah because he thought, "Surely the fear of God is not in this place" (Gen. 20:11, KJV). Consequently, they would have no qualms about killing him to get his wife. To say, "There is no respect for God in this place," waters down the meaning almost beyond recognition. If you have respect for God, you may take your hat off in church, or you may forgo swearing. If you respect someone, you think highly of him and are polite. But if you fear God, you do what is right at all costs.

One can understand why Christians are ill at ease with the phrase "the fear of the Lord." Surely "perfect love casts out fear" (1 John 4:18, NASB). Therefore, if we have really come to know God's love for us in Christ and have responded with our own love, it would appear that "the fear of the Lord" no longer has any valid meaning for us. However, if we study the context of the above verse, it becomes clear that John is describing a fear which is *terror*, the trepidation that at any moment, for any reason, God is going to drop us into the gaping jaws of hell. As we have said, this is not the fear of the Lord.

Two other Old Testament verses help us to understand the meaning of the phrase. "The fear of the Lord is the beginning of knowledge" (Prov. 1:7, KJV). Only when we have knelt in awe before God's glory, His greatness, His total otherness from Creation, are we in a position to discover in the deepest sense, what life is about. But if we drag God down to our level to explain Him and His works, we can never come to the truth.

The second verse is from the Psalms: "The friendship of the Lord is for those who fear Him" (Ps. 25:14, RSV). On the surface, that seems a very strange statement. Surely, friendship and fear are incompatible. And yet friendship is based upon mutual understanding. And any correct understanding of God must take into account who He really is—His eternity, His infinity, His utter reality, all of which would consume us in a moment. Only when we have seen Him as Isaiah did and can cry out, "I am ruined," are we in a position to appreciate the wonder of His love and move into the glory of its blaze.

Thus the fear of the Lord is that appropriate awe and wonder of Him which will shape all we do. It is the necessary precursor to appreciating His love. It is the essential continuing ingredient that will prevent our love from turning into a patronizing affection.

Love of God as Father, awe of God as Master—these are what will motivate us to live in a way that truly exemplifies His worth. Too little of either one has a negative effect. Because awe without love is cold and lifeless, one is tempted to do only enough to get by. Because love without awe becomes flabby and sentimental, one is tempted to dwell on the good feeling, and use God to maintain that feeling. But together they balance each other and wing us forward. Awe will never use God. Love will never ask, "How little can I do to get by?" Together they are like skeleton and flesh, each complementing the other. No blind lambs for the person possessing these.

Oh God, forgive me for trying to buy You with cheap offerings.
Do something for me that will make me want to give the best.

6
WHO HAS A
PERFECT LAMB?

"Oh, that one of you would shut the temple doors, so that you would not light useless fires on My altar! I am not pleased with you," says the Lord Almighty, "and I will accept no offering from your hands.

"My name will be great among the nations, from the rising to the setting of the sun. In every place incense and pure offerings will be brought to My name, because My name will be great among the nations," says the Lord Almighty.

"But you profane it by saying of the Lord's table, 'It is defiled,' and of its food, 'It is contemptible.' And you say, 'What a burden!' and you sniff at it contemptuously," says the Lord Almighty.

"When you bring injured, crippled, or diseased animals and offer them as sacrifices, should I accept them from your hands?" says the Lord. "Cursed is the cheat who has an acceptable male in his flock and vows to give it, but then sacrifices a blemished animal to the Lord. For I am a great King," says the Lord Almighty, "and My name is to be feared among the nations."

Malachi 1:10-14

If we have accurate knowledge of God's moral perfection, of His infinite power and endless love, we will give Him the perfect offering which He deserves. But why all this stress upon keeping the Law perfectly? Why did God make such demands on the Old Testament believers? And what does that have to do with 20th-century Christians?

The nature of our offerings and our reasons for giving them have everything to do with the vitality of our relationship to God. If we can correctly understand the purpose and meaning of the Old Testament offerings, we will be in a position to make our own right offerings and to know the satisfying closeness with God which results.

The Law

Some scholars have argued that the concern of Ezra, Nehemiah, Malachi, and others for careful keeping of the law is a kind of "hardening of the arteries" of Judaism. It is seen as a defect which issued in a pharisaism that spent all its energies straining gnats out of camel soup!

And to be sure, there were Jews who went careening out of one ditch and into the other. They said, "Ah, now we see it! God sent us into exile because we broke His law. Well, never again. We'll keep every last one." But in doing so, they forgot the purpose of the law. It did not exist as a means of making them acceptable to God. It was not a ladder to glory.

● The law was meant to be a schoolmaster (Gal. 3:24) to show them the nature of God. The Hebrew word, "*Torah*" means "instruction" or "teaching." It is because of this teaching function that the law was to be kept perfectly. If it were kept in a sloppy or a haphazard way, its whole function would be jeopardized. One of the ways in which the law taught spiritual truth was through object lessons. How does a child get hold of such an abstract truth as $2 + 2 = 4$? Through an object lesson in which he adds two objects to two other objects.

How does a spiritual child learn the truth that there are certain attitudes and behaviors which defile one in the presence of the Pure and Clean? Through an object lesson. God said, "There are clean animals and unclean animals. Don't eat the unclean ones." So every time they sat down to a meal, the Jews confronted the distinction between clean and unclean. By the time Christ came, the people should have gotten the point. As He said, "Not what enters into the mouth defiles the man, but what proceeds out of the mouth, this defiles the man" (Matt. 15:11, NASB).

● A second reason for absolute adherence to the law was to teach the seriousness of sin. In pagan society sin was regrettable but not serious, because you couldn't help yourself. It was merely the result of being a miserable, finite human. And at any rate, what was sin to one deity was commendable to another. If you wore green to please the Green God, you were sure to incur the wrath of the Orange God.

But sin is much more than simply doing something which a god doesn't like, or something which is tinged with finitude. Sin is an offense against our own natures and the very nature of creation. As human beings, we were made to a certain pattern. To fail to follow the pattern set out for us is to sin and thus to offend all creation.

Their extreme adherence to the law should have enabled the Judeans to begin to understand the real nature of sin which was tied into the nature of man. Sin is a rebellion against the way we were created. If there ever was to be a remedy for sin, it would have to be built on a recognition of the seriousness of the disease. The requirements of absolute adherence to the law helped to produce that recognition.

● But there is yet another reason why the law was to be adhered to precisely. It is especially pertinent to the problem referred to in Malachi. The law, and especially the prescribed offerings, show us Christ. What does it take to remove sin—this cancer in the body of the universe? Can God simply close His eyes and say, 'We'll act as if that never happened''? Not if He is sustainer of a universe where every sufficient cause produces a predictable effect. For Him to simply ignore sin would break the whole consistency on which the Creation depends.

Sin is a matter of life and death. We cannot toss God a little bribe to forget the whole thing. When a Hebrew brought an offering, he put his hands on that perfect, innocent lamb's head, and said over and over, "My sin costs a life, an innocent, spotless life."

Across the centuries, how much innocent blood has cascaded down that altar onto the temple pavement! Morning and evening on normal days, and ever so much more on feast days, it poured down. Josephus, the Jewish historian, tells us that in Roman times up to 250,000 lambs were slain on Passover Day! There had to be special gutters to carry the blood away into the Kidron Brook. Jesus waded through that bloody stream on His way to Gethsemane. And through the pre-

Christian years, as sensitive Jews viewed the endless parade of doomed animals, some of them must have cried out, "How can an animal carry my sins? Oh, what can wash away my sins?" And the voice of God whispered across eternity, "He is coming!"

How insulting, then, were the Judeans' blind and crippled offerings! They shouted to the skies what the Judeans really thought of God, of sin, of the coming Redeemer, and of themselves. "You sniff at Me," God said. What an eloquent phrase! Gestures of contempt vary around the world, but we Americans have one very like what is being referred to here. Someone says, "What do you think of So and So?" If we wish to express utter disregard we merely puff a little air through our noses. We sniff, indicating that the person in question is worth nothing more. About God, the Judeans were saying, "He, the Lord of glory, is worth our cast-offs, nothing more." No wonder the Prophet cried out for someone with moral courage to shut the doors of the temple and stop this mockery. Better no offering at all than a worthless thing which makes us feel pious while degrading God.

Internal Law

You may be thinking, "We live in the age of grace. Since Christ has come we are not under the law anymore. How does all this apply to us?" To be sure, the pharisaic idea of law-keeping is false. External performance is not the main issue in obedience to God. But the Old Testament does not teach this anyway. It puts much more weight on external performance than the New Testament does, since the nature of the law as an object lesson demands this. But the Old Testament always points beyond the external to the internal. Circumcision was meaningless without circumcision of the heart (Deut. 30:6). The sacrifice acceptable to God is a broken and a contrite heart (Ps. 51:17). "Even though you offer me your burnt offerings and cereal offerings, I will not accept them. . . . But let justice roll down like waters, and righteousness like an everflowing stream" (Amos 5:22, 24, RSV).

The external performance was to provide a vehicle and a stimulus for the expression of the internal. The problem with the Pharisees was not that they did too much; it was that they didn't do enough! They didn't internalize the meaning of their performance. Thus Jesus said to His disciples, "Unless your righteousness surpasses that of the scribes and Pharisees, you shall not enter the kingdom of heaven" (Matt. 5:20, NASB).

Much of the ceremonial law served its purpose and we are free of it. Much of the specific civil law does not apply to modern urban life, although its principles are still the foundation of our civil code.

But the moral code, as exemplified in the Ten Commandments, still stands before us, saying, "If you are the children of God, then you will live out your Father's character, and this is it." And our conformity to the Father's character is always tested by the physical evidence in our lives. To say, "Well, God looks on the heart, so it doesn't matter whether I attend church, pray regularly, give substantial amounts of my income, or live by unquestionable ethics" is a dodge.

I wear a wedding band. That wedding band does not make me married. In fact, the marriage license does not even make me married. For marriage is a spiritual thing, a thing of the heart. If I need to take that ring off while doing heavy work with my hands, nothing is harmed. But if the first thing I do when leaving town on a business trip is to put that silver circle in my pocket, and not put it on again until just before I walk in the door on my return, you know something about my spirit. The external and the internal are inextricably linked in human thought and behavior, and we need to stop behaving as if they can be separated.

Obedience

This truth has another side. How often young people, and many not so young, say, "Well, I'm not going to go to church because I don't feel like it and I don't want to lie to God. I know He wants me to be honest." How good it feels to be so righteous! But what a farce! If we will obey with our bodies, our spirits are going to come along! And obedience rendered contrary to our feelings is worth much more than obedience given only because something feels good. When our primary motive is to feel good, our obedience costs nothing. How glad I am that John Wesley did what he did not want to do but felt he should, as he "went very unwillingly to a society in Aldersgate." While he was there, Wesley came to the assurance of his salvation, something he had been seeking for 20 years. Because of Wesley's obedience, God was able to change the character of England and America, through him and his brother Charles.

This coupling of the spiritual and the physical was seen in the nature of the animal required for the Old Testament offering. In the days before artificial insemination, the future of every farmer's flock or herd, and thus his own financial future, depended upon his ability to raise healthy young males to sire offspring. They kept the best and got rid of the worst. Thus, God was asking those Judeans to commit their future to Him, not just in words but in deeds. The man and woman who sacrificed the *best* of this year's crop of rams had "put their money where their mouths were." This is obedience. This is trust. On the other hand, refusal to give the best was a statement of distrust of God and dependence on self.

God does not wish obedience from dull and unwilling hearts. His will is that we will each know the overwhelming assurance of His love, and like Isaiah, will enthusiastically say, "God, here I am. What can I do?" No longer, "How little can I do? How far from You can I live, and still make it to glory?" Now it is, "How much can I do? How close can I live?"

In his book *Love Is Now*, Peter Gillquist tells of a college student who was being encouraged by two friends to accept Christ. He told them he really wanted to but couldn't, because he would have to witness, and just knew he couldn't do that. His friends shared with him the truth that you don't *have* to do anything but accept Christ. He said, "Well, if you promise me that Christ will come into my life today and that I'll never have to witness, I'll accept Him." They promised and he prayed to receive Christ. Then they talked with him about his forgiveness from all his sin and his new life in Christ.

This is the most fantastic thing I've ever heard. I can't believe that I didn't have to do anything to get it. He walked over to the fraternity house. It was about 10:00 in the morning. He approached the first friend he saw and said, "I've got to tell you the most amazing thing I have ever heard. Today I realized that I could invite Jesus Christ to come into my life, and that I wouldn't have to witness or do anything, and He'd still come in. This is the greatest thing I have ever heard. Isn't that fantastic!" and by evening, he had spread the word around the entire fraternity. Because he didn't *have* to.

This is what Malachi was talking about. Must we give the perfect sacrifice in order to *earn* God's love? No, we can never earn it. But if we have ever received that love, truly received it, we will want to give our best. This is exactly what Paul said to the Galatian Christians: "Don't fall into the trap of saying, 'I'm a Christian; I must do this.' That's legalism and will kill you. But live by the Spirit. Surrender yourselves totally to His Spirit of love and then you will fulfill the law as God's character is manifested in your life." (See Galatians 5.)

The Judeans were saying, "Well, we've got to do it, but we hate it." So their service was sloppy and contemptuous, and it nauseated God. It was as if an empty glass were griping, "I've got to overflow." Never. The only way a glass can overflow is to be placed under a running faucet. Then it can overflow *and* cease from its own labors.

Why did the Judeans have so little sense of God's presence? Why did the apparent injustices and contradictions of life loom so large? Why was their religion a drag and a drudgery? Because they would not surrender themselves to accept the limitless love of the Lord of hosts. They insisted on trying to use Him to serve their purposes. When He didn't bless them, they said, "God, You're not worth it," and did even less.

But even if we will not respond to God's love, others will. This happened to the Jews who watched with horror as Gentiles fell in love with Jesus, a Jew who claimed to be the fulfillment of all that the Jewish Scriptures taught. The Jews said, "This is *our* God! They can't just take Him over like that!" But He wasn't *their* God. He is not anybody's private possession. He goes where He may be Himself, redeeming, releasing, and revitalizing people.

We are seeing a similar happening today. For 150 years England and America have been *the* Christian nations to send out missionaries to all the world. But in the latter half of the 20th century, Christianity is less and less potent in these two nations. In their place, the peoples of Africa are surging to Christ. We are told that if the present rate of growth continues until the year 2,000, Africa will be the most Christian continent in the world. "But, Lord, those people are just heathens. They're uncivilized. They don't understand how to govern themselves, etc.!'' To which the Lord replies, ''My name is great among the nations. . . . But you profane it. They love Me; they fear Me. Do you?''

Oh God, where are You?
''I am wherever people will surrender their futures to My love and render Me the honor due My name.''

III
THE COVENANT
OF GOD

7
ARE YOU IN COVENANT WITH GOD?

At times you attempt to use God for your convenience. You give Him just the minimum you think necessary, to keep Him from upsetting your plans. We all do this.

Malachi suggests that an inadequate understanding of God is one reason. We neither appreciate the depth of His love nor feel proper awe for His greatness. We just don't know Him very well.

But why don't we know Him? Why didn't the Judeans know Him? After all, He had been revealing Himself directly to them for nearly 1,400 years. And what about us who have seen the light of God in the face of Christ? Why don't we know Him well enough to give ourselves in grateful service to Him?

The second chapter of Malachi probes into the reason for this ignorance. When we take a careful look at this chapter, we see one word being repeated six times. If I tell my young son four times to "Sit down!" he would be quite correct in assuming it would be wise for him to do what I say. The same principle is true in literature. Repetition marks a key thought.

The repeated word here in Malachi 2 is *covenant*, appearing in verses, 4, 5, 8, 10, 14. The idea of the covenant was at the heart of Israel's relation to God. The covenant bond between God and Israel set her off from neighboring nations and was perfectly suited for revealing the unique character of the one God.

Across the years as God had watched people create gods in their own image, He longed to show them who He really was. Their speculations had so led them astray that any revelation within the prevailing religous forms of the day would only have compounded the confusion. Even more serious was a misconception, going all the way back to Eden, that God was not to be trusted. That He was playing His own game and was quite willing to use persons to achieve His own ends. Thus religion had become an attempt to beat deity at its own game: manipulate the gods before they can manipulate you.

The Suzerainty Covenant

So how was God to show the world that He was trustworthy, that He could not be manipulated, and that there were absolute standards by which the world was made to operate? He stepped outside of their religious forms and used an idea from the political arena, the covenant, and particularly the suzerainty covenant.

This was an agreement between a great king and a subject nation. In such a covenant the king agreed to protect and support the subject, while the subject agreed to do certain things and to refrain from doing others. The written covenant was kept in a special place and was to be read publicly at stated times. What was there about this form which made it appropriate to what God wanted to do?

● The covenant was an ideal teaching model to promote monotheism. Typically, such a covenant stressed that the subject nation would recognize no other kings. Its commitment was to one king only. If the Hebrews were bound by a covenant not to recognize any other god, they would soon realize that there *is* no other God.

● The covenant gave God an opportunity to prove Himself trustworthy. A king bound himself in a covenant to do certain things in the care and building up of his subjects. How amazed the Hebrews must have been when they realized that God was committing Himself in this way. He was putting His name on the line. No other god would do that. Was this one different? Would this one keep His promises?

● The covenant generally stressed obedience of an ethical and moral nature as an appropriate response to a king's character. If a subject wanted a king to protect and help him, then he had to do those things which would please the king. How well-suited this was to God's plans. Humans had gone astray in believing they could establish their own ethical and moral foundations. How could God show them that as they were made in His image, His own moral nature set the only standard within which life can be lived happily? He could do it through the covenant. Since the Hebrews were to be subject to Him and Him alone, His character was the standard they were to measure up to.

● The covenant form, especially as adapted by God, emphasized grace and love. The relationship did not come into being *after* the subjects performed the stipulations. Rather, the relationship was dependent on some previous historic event. In the case of the Hebrews, the deliverance from Egypt was that event. God had not said, "Keep the law perfectly and then I'll think about delivering you." No, He had delivered them solely on the basis of grace. The relationship had been entered into when the Hebrews accepted God's gracious power. Only later did the formal covenant—and especially the parts we call the law—spell out how they needed to live to preserve this gracious relationship.

The covenant is God's way of teaching the truth about Himself in everyday life. There is only one God and He intends to bless us. Indeed, the only thing which prevents His blessing is our failure to live in God's intended way of life.

And how the Hebrews delighted in their covenant. How good of God to show them what life was about, to show how they were made to live, and to shed the light of His counsel on their dark paths. This was one of the reasons the Israelites felt superior to their pagan neighbors. The pagans were groping in darkness for life's meaning while the Hebrews had found it—had found *Him*.

The truth of the covenant remains just as vital today as then. Our first need is not a philosophy book to answer our questions about life and God. We first need a surrender, then a relationship, and then a life. If our problem were primarily intellectual—if lack of knowledge prevented us from living successfully—the philosophy book might help us. But our problem is not lack of knowledge, just as Adam and Eve's wasn't. They knew all they needed to know, and yet they chose a way which destined all of us to destruction.

The problem is one of the will. Until our wills are brought into submission and we enter into a relation of obedience with our Creator, our understanding of Him will always be dim. Only as we live out His nature in our own flesh will we begin to taste and know the wonders of His purity and integrity, His faithfulness and love.

Sealing the Covenant

But what if the subject nation would not keep the covenant? When the covenant was sealed, the two parties to the agreement walked between the two halves of a sacrificial animal and said, "May God do so to me if I don't keep this covenant!" (See Jeremiah 34:18-19.) They swore to be faithful to the agreement and solemnly asked God to kill them if they broke it.

At Sinai, Moses called the people to hear the covenant read, and to commit themselves to it. The people immediately said yes, they would. After all, why not? God had delivered them from Egypt with signs and wonders and now wanted to be their God. Of course. It is as though the perennial wallflower, having fallen into the swimming pool through her own clumsiness, finds the most handsome boy at the party saving her and asking her to be his girl! Sure, they would enter into the covenant! (See Exodus 24.)

Did they know what they were committing themselves to? Probably not. We usually don't. Which of us really understood our marriage vows? We might have been afraid to make the commitment, if we had. But many of us, by Christ's grace, can say we're very glad we did it and glad it involved vows of that seriousness.

Hearing the people's affirmation, Moses took the blood from 12 sacrificed bulls and divided it in half. Then he said, "Behold the blood of the covenant," and threw one half on the altar and the other half on the people. What was he doing? The ceremony by which a covenant was sealed involved the two parties linking arms and walking between the two halves of a sacrificed animal (Gen. 15:9-21; Jer. 34:18-19). As they did so, they called on God to strike them dead (like the animal) if they broke the covenant. Since God and the people could not physically walk between the halves, the throwing of the blood on the altar and on the people symbolized that act. God and the people called a divine curse on themselves if they failed to keep the covenant.

I wonder if the seriousness of what they were doing came home to them as the blood ran down their faces. Maybe a shiver went up their spines as they murmured, "What have we gotten ourselves into?"

Well might they shiver, for within a few weeks they would be dancing around a golden calf, breaking their glorious covenant into meaninglessness. And while it would be comforting to be able to say "Yes, but they never broke it again," the fact is that apart from a few notable exceptions, the rest of the Old Testament is a melancholy story of tragedy. Again and again, the Hebrews betrayed the very thing which made them a people. The covenant stood over against them in all its glory and condemned them. Their hearts attested its loveliness, but their wills defied it.

Hesed

God would have been fully just, had He destroyed every one of them and forgotten the whole endeavor. But one of the features of the covenant was *hesed*. The two parties to a covenant swore to do *hesed* with one another. There is no single English word which captures the whole meaning of this concept. Such words as love, mercy, lovingkindness, grace, steadfast love, and faithfulness have been employed by various translators to convey some of its meaning. The central idea is "passionate loyalty." The two parties swear to be loyal to each other in every circumstance, to defend each other against all attacks, both physical and verbal, to support each other and resolutely think the best of each other, come what may. This is what David and Jonathan swore to each other, and this is what accounts for David's searching out Mephibosheth (2 Sam. 9) to care for him, when any other shaky new monarch would have ruthlessly squashed the crippled remnant of the opposition family.

The Hebrews discovered that God's *hesed* is everlasting! He continued to do *hesed* with them long after they had shattered their side of the agreement. What sort of God was this? He was not only trustworthy but persistently trustworthy! He was not only loving but insistently loving! It was embarrassing. Had He no pride? Slowly, ever so slowly, the Hebrew people realized they had not found God, but God had found *them* and the His very nature was *hesed*. He *wanted* to give them the good things they needed. They did not have to manipulate Him to produce those things. Indeed, they could not. Rather, He would pour them out in superabundance if the people would do one thing: surrender their own destructive dominance of their lives and live in trusting obedience.

Yet how deep the human problem runs! It seemed that for every Hebrew who learned the secret of life, ten others slipped farther away. Though the lessons of the wilderness years finally made their impact and Israel was able to receive God's gift of the land, the memory lasted barely a generation. The sorry pictures of the Book of Judges remind us of Paul's words, ''Ever learning, yet never coming to a knowledge of the truth.'' How many times they saw that God's abundance was theirs, if they would only entrust the strings of their lives to Him. Yet, once the crisis was past they slipped right back. Like the rest of us, they would give Him anything if He would just keep His hands off the controls!

The God of the covenant is as much at the heart of our Christian faith as He was at the heart of Israel's faith. He invites us to experience the benefits of His commitment to us, as we commit ourselves to Him. He means to teach us the realities of grace, of sufficiency and of righteousness, as we live them out in lives of trust and dependence.

Yet how easy it is for us, like the Judeans, to say, ''Yes, Lord, I am fully committed to You. Why aren't You blessing me? Why don't I know these realities in my life?'' The issue is this: Am I in covenant with God? Am I genuinely committed to Him? Or have I, like the Hebrews, simply run some pretty words over my tongue?

Oh Lord, we believe You are faithful. We want to experience that faithfulness. We admit that it is all too easy to say ''Sure, we'll serve You,'' without ever meaning to do those things—or to let You do those things—which will make our commitment real. Have mercy on us.

8
WHERE DO YOU FIND LIFE AND PEACE?

"And now this admonition is for you, O priests. If you do not listen, and if you do not set your heart to honor My name," says the Lord Almighty, "I will send a curse upon you, and I will curse your blessings. Yes, I have already cursed them, because you have not set your heart to honor Me.

"Because of you I will rebuke your descendants; I will spread on your faces the offal from your festival sacrifices, and you will be carried off with it. And you will know that I have sent you this admonition so that My covenant with Levi may continue," says the Lord Almighty.

"My covenant was with him, a covenant of life and peace, and I gave them to him; this called for reverence and he revered Me and stood in awe of My name. True instruction was in his mouth and nothing false was found on his lips. He walked with Me in peace and uprightness, and turned many from sin.

"For the lips of a priest ought to preserve knowledge, and from his mouth men should seek instruction—because he is the messenger of the Lord Almighty. But you have turned from the way and by your teaching have caused many to stumble; you have violated the covenant with Levi," says the Lord Almighty. "So I have caused you to be despised and humiliated before all the people, because you have not followed my ways but have shown partiality in matters of the law."

Malachi 2:1-9

You test the reality of your commitment to live in covenant with God by evaluating the level of commitment to the lesser covenants of your life. It was the Apostle John who said, "Don't tell me you love God, whom you can't see, when you hate your brother, whom you can see." (See 1 John 4:20.) It is somewhat futile to talk about your healthy commitment to God if your face-to-face commitments are diseased. On the other hand, if your earthly covenants are in good order, how much easier it is to do those things which are necessary to cement the covenant with God.

An examination of Judah's relations yielded a grim result. Three covenants were investigated and all three were found to be broken. The first is the covenant of Levi (Mal. 2:1-9); the second is the covenant of the fathers (10-12); and the third, the covenant with the wife of your youth (13-16). The picture which emerges is of a people unable, or unwilling, to commit themselves to anything or anyone.

Covenant of Levi

The first covenant referred to the priests, the religous leaders of the nation. When Malachi addressed the priests he spoke of the covenant of Levi. What did he mean by this? If you remember, Levi was one of the 12 sons of Jacob. His descendants were made the custodians of the religious life of the Hebrew people (Num. 3—4; Deut. 18:1–19). The family tree looked like this:

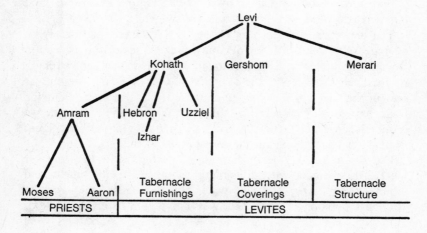

While the descendants of Aaron were the priests, the rest of Levi's family also had a significant role in the religious life of Israel. In the wilderness years they were responsible for moving and caring for the tabernacle. After the settlement they assumed more varied functions as they located in various parts of the country. But all of these functions were related to preserving and deepening Israel's understanding of herself as the people of God.

God had made an agreement with the family of Levi. If they would be faithful in their leadership of the people, He would see that all their needs were met. If they would loyally serve both God and man, they might enjoy positions of authority and importance in the community.

The task of the priesthood was two-fold, but both aspects served one function: they were the mediators, the go-betweens. On the one hand, they served to bring humans to God. When a human being had sinned and alienated himself from God, then the priest was empowered to say, "There is a way back. The record can be cleared. Here, let me help you." This is the aspect of the priesthood we know best.

But there is another, lesser known aspect. If the priest was detailed to bring humans to God, he was also called to bring God to humans. This was the teaching function. Every generation had to learn all over again who God was. As we said before, that happened when the covenant was lived out. As people lived according to the stipulations of that agreement, they learned by concrete example what sort of God this was and what sorts of persons they were.

The importance of teaching in the Old Testament can hardly be overstressed. One of the most beautiful examples of this is seen in Deuteronomy 6. Loving God with all one's heart, soul, and strength meant an absorption with the character of God. That absorption was seen in obedience to His commandments. Then somewhere along the line, the younger generation would ask, "Wait a minute! Why do we do all this, anyway?" That was the opportunity for the priest or parent to begin to tell them about the mighty acts of this great God.

One of the lovely places where this occurred was at the Passover meal. After the meal with all its rich symbolism of lamb, unleavened bread, bitter herbs, and salt water, the youngest child—or the youngest person present, if it was not a family group—asked,

"Father, why do we do this?" Then the ancient story was told again; how God had met them in their anguish, when they were slaves, and had delivered them with mighty power to make them a nation of priests to Himself.

And how does one remember God? By doing! In the Old Testament remembering was never a strictly mental activity. If I truly remember, then I do what He says. And if I do not do what He says, it is plain that I do *not* remember His greatness and power and love, no matter what I *say* I remember. Once more this is evidence that the spiritual and the physical are inseparable.

Thus it was the responsibility of the priesthood to so teach, and live, and enforce the Law so that each succeeding generation came to an experiential knowledge of God. They were indeed the messengers of the Lord of hosts (2:7). They in themselves were to be the message of God's love and power, grace, and faithfulness. Their lives were to embody the truth they taught. Because they knew God, others would know Him by looking at them. If the priesthood failed at this crucial point, their failure would infect the whole nation in a matter of two or three generations.

Covenant of Life and Peace

God's special covenant with the family of Levi was a covenant of life and peace. At the end of Psalm 23, we read that goodness and mercy will *pursue* us so long as life shall last. In the same way, life and peace were just waiting to fall upon the family of Levi. All too often we feel we must labor and struggle and do everything letter perfectly in order to receive a small taste of the blessings. Not so! God is waiting for us to meet the very minimum conditions. Then He will pour out all His abundance!

What does it mean to be alive? Two bums stood on a street corner watching a funeral cortege go by. The hearse was so shiny it hurt their eyes to look at it; it was so long they couldn't look at the front and back fenders at the same time; gorgeous flowers were massed around the casket. As the hearse turned a corner and drove out of sight, one bum nudged the other and said, "Man, that's living!"

All too often, we confuse living with dying. We look at a profusion of possessions and creature comforts and say, "That's living." We look at prestige, influence, and power and say, "That's living." We look at people whose spiritual lives are being steadily squashed under the interests and effects of this physical world, and we say they're alive. But they're dying!

The rich young ruler ran to Jesus to ask Him how to find life. Did Jesus give him some hot financial tips? Did He show him where to find the newest inn? No. He told him that the only way for him to live was to get out from under his possessions. He said in another place, "A man's real life in no way depends upon the number of his possessions" (Luke 12:15, PH).

Oh, to be alive! To be free of the lust for power, position, and things—a lust which ruins every day because it can never be satisfied. To be free to love, to give, to cherish without needing to possess. To be free to have integrity, honor, and purity and not to find any price too high for these. To be free to be human, neither hating nor deifying humanity. Just to be myself today, alive in the power of the risen Jesus.

> Heav'n above is softer blue,
> Earth around is sweeter green!
> Something lives in every hue
> Christless eyes have never seen;
> Birds with gladder songs o'erflow,
> Flow'rs with deeper beauties shine,
> Since I know, as now I know,
> I am His, and He is mine.
>
> George Wade Robinson

A covenant of peace. All the world seeks peace yet never finds it. For peace seems to be "something out there." But that isn't right. For peace is "something in here." In the Old Testament, the word *shalom*, normally translated "peace," has a deeper meaning—"completeness, health, harmony, wholeness, and integration." In the language of today, to have *shalom* is "to have it all together." That's what we want, a sense of being a unified person, of living an integrated life, of going in a clear direction. But this is possible only when the walls between us and God are broken down. For the world cannot put Humpty Dumpty together again. It can only break him into smaller and smaller pieces.

A Broken Covenant

Life and peace. Those are what God offered in turn for the priest's faithful mediation between Him and humanity. But what happened? The priests broke the covenant. And how early it happened! Already in the Book of Judges we read of Levites engaging in idolatry and extramarital sexual liaisons. By the time of Samuel, the Aaronic priests themselves were corrupt. The sons of the high priest Eli were accustomed to taking the best portions of the sacrifices for themselves, demanding extra money for performing a sacrifice, lying with the women who served at the entrance to the tabernacle, and more. "The sons of Eli were worthless men; they did not know the Lord" (1 Sam. 2:12, NASB). And their precedent seems to have carried down through the years; for Hosea, speaking around 750 B.C., some 300 years after Samuel, said,

> "My contention is with you, O priest. . . . My people are destroyed for lack of knowledge; because you have rejected knowledge, I reject you from being a priest to me. And since you have forgotten the law of your God, I will also forget your children. The more they increased, the more they sinned against me; I will change their glory into shame" (Hosea 4:4-7, RSV).

How quickly we human beings miss what matters in life and sell the priceless to buy the cheap. We take advantage of a position of privilege and responsibility to use it for selfish ends, instead of using it to build up those in our care.

Now you may be thinking, "Boy, that's right! It's the preachers' fault. If they would just do their job, the church wouldn't be in the mess it is today." I have disquieting news for you. As Protestants, we believe in the priesthood of *all* believers. That covenant now exists with all of us, and we are all called upon to be mediators—to offer the Lamb to those whose sin separates them from God, and to teach the church and the world of the true nature of God. Surely, those of us who make our living through some form of Christian ministry bear a heavy responsibility for the present state of the church, but *every*

Christian is a minister. What are you doing to fulfill *your* covenant obligations?

Have you ever known church leaders who used their position for their own glory, their own ends, their own purposes? God has ordained positions of authority and the commensurate honor that goes with them. That is good and necessary. But how easy it is to succumb to Satan's whisper, "Heaven knows you've earned this position and you certainly work hard in it. It's all right to get a little glory for yourself out of this. Go right ahead." And in fact, if there does not appear to us to be an amount of glory equal to the job's tedium or difficulty, it is all too easy to dodge the responsibility.

Have you ever known Christians who used their own religious attainments—their God-given measure of life and peace—as a means of achieving glory for themselves? How we love to be known as "great" Christians. The bitterest words Jesus ever spoke were directed at some of the most "righteous" people in the Jewish community—the Pharisees. "Watch out for the teachers of the law. They like to walk around in flowing robes and be greeted in the marketplace, and have the most important seats . . . and have the places of honor" (Mark 12:38-39).

How good it feels to be known, to stand out in a crowd! In his powerful essay, "The Inner Ring," C.S. Lewis speaks of the horror we have of being unknown, and of the delicious feeling of being on a first-name basis with "those who count." Think what it did for a teacher's ego to walk down the street and have people call out, "Good morning, Rabbi, my great one." And after all, why shouldn't they be honored—they prayed such moving prayers! Anybody who could pray like that must be quite a believer. No wonder Jesus said, "They already have the reward they want."

But why did He warn, "Watch out for them"? Because they devoured widows' houses. When I was a child, that phrase conjured up very strange pictures. I saw a big, mean Pharisee taking a huge bite out of a poor widow's house. The reality is far worse than my childish misconception. But what is the connection between loving to be admired as a righteous person and being a cold-eyed forecloser of mortgages? It's pretty straightforward, when you think about it. These people had gotten all their religious attainments for themselves, through strict adherence to the law. Therefore, they expected to apply the law just as coldly to everybody else. Never having experienced grace for themselves, they had none to apply to others.

When personal glory becomes the motivating factor in our lives, a very strange unplugging of our ethical faculties follows. Number One so fills our field of vision that we simply can't see how we use other people. When we think we can use God to advance our ends, using people becomes perfectly natural. And unfortunately, the stories are too common to the "Christian" who keeps a Bible on his desk but is as compassionate as a bulldozer toward anyone in his way.

Judgment

God said through Malachi, "I will rebuke your offspring" (v. 3). The same theme was brought out by Hosea. And it has happened. The Jewish priesthood is incredibly confused today. Nobody knows for sure who is a son of Aaron. Many claim that descent, but there is little possibility of proving it. The whole priesthood has disintegrated. No *shalom* here. When we believe our attainments are ours to do with as we wish, they begin to drift away from us like smoke through gauze. They are covenant gifts, not permanent possessions.

"I will spread dung upon your faces, the dung of your offerings" (v. 3). It is as if God said, "OK, you want earthly glory, power, privilege, praise. Here take all you want, and one day you will see it for what it is—dung." I wonder if Paul had this passage in mind when he penned Philippians. He said, "I had it all. I had every gain it was possible to make. My record was spotless. Right by geneology, right by religion, right by the particular brand of my religion, right by my personal attainments within that brand. Right? No—wrong. It was all manure. All worthless. Why? Because it built me up and put Christ down. It made me believe a lie—that I needed God's help occasionally, not His unconditional grace continually." (See Philippians 3.)

The nation of Israel was in the state it was because those who could have led it into God's grace and glory had instead opted for their own glory. They had taken God's free and abundant gifts and perverted them to their own selfish ends. Even worse, they took credit for what God had given! And for what? Earthly glory. In all the world, there is nothing so transitory as earthly glory. The coach whose team of two years ago had a 13-0 record was hailed as a genius in the motivation and training of men. This year his team has an 0-13 record and he is the world's greatest idiot. What is so fickle as glory? She envelops us just long enough for us to develop an unrelenting thirst for her, and then flounces off to throw her arms around our unworthy neighbor.

The Weighty Glory

By contrast, the glory which God wants to share with us is not fickle, ephemeral, or transitory. In fact, the Hebrew word translated "glory" comes from a root which means "heavy, weighty, solid." Its basic meaning is the very opposite of that which characterizes earthly glory. How can the two concepts be so opposite?

The contrast has to do with the character of God. Do you remember that when God came into the tabernacle, His glory filled the place? (Ex. 40:34) The glory was the manifestation of the presence of God. When John spoke of Jesus as the Incarnation, he called Him the glory of God (John 1:14; 17:1-5). God's glory is His presence, and it is as real and as unchanging as He is Himself. The wonder of God's love is that He wants to share His glory with us. "For this slight momentary affliction is preparing for us an eternal weight of glory beyond all comparison" (2 Cor. 4:17, RSV). He wants to make us real, solid, dependable—persons with integrity. That is God's glory.

But the only way in which you and I may experience God's glory in our lives is to surrender to Him our lust for earthly fame, prestige, and honor which tempts us to surrender realities for appearances, gold for tinsel. Which will it be: a glory which is solely external and passes away, or a glory which lives within and becomes more real with every passing day?

To be sure, it is hard to wait. It is hard to commit ourselves unreservedly, and turn our backs on the lovely gauzy veils Satan offers us, in favor of something which is being ever so slowly chiseled out, so slowly that it will never be fully seen this side of eternity.

"But we know that when He shall appear we shall be like Him" (1 John 3:2, KJV). Being like Him, sharing the glory of His reality, that's worth waiting for.

Where are You, God? In me? Wanting to share Your reality with the world? Through me?

9
DID YOU MARRY
IN THE FAITH?

*Have we not all one Father? Did not one God create us? Why do
we profane the covenant of our fathers by breaking faith with one
another?*

*Judah has broken faith. A detestable thing has been committed
in Israel and in Jerusalem: Judah has desecrated the sanctuary
the Lord loves, by marrying the daughter of a foreign god. As for
the man who does this, whoever he may be, may the Lord cut him
off from the tents of Jacob—even though he brings offerings to
the Lord Almighty.*

Malachi 2:10-12

Why was Judah in the condition it was in 440 B.C.? Why is America
in the condition it is today? One answer for both times is that the
people who could be the mediators between God and broken people—
the priests of old and clergy of today—have chosen their own glory
and have broken their covenant with God to find that glory.

But Malachi offers yet a second cause for the problem. He adjusts
the focus of his laser beam to include not only the religious leadership,
but the people as a whole. Some have argued that he is speaking of all
people everywhere since God is everyone's Father. But a careful
reading of these three verses makes it clear that Judah is the people he
is addressing, and that Abraham is the father through whose covenant
they are brothers and sisters.

So what was the people's state? The picture was grim. They had broken faith. They had betrayed a trust. With God? Ultimately, yes, but that's not the point here. They had been faithless to one another! When I fail to keep covenant with God, when I cannot bear the risk of leaving my life in His hands, and fall back to the insecurity of manipulating it myself, I am faithless to *you*!

We Christians often have the feeling, "My responsibility is to God. I'll do my best to live for Him and, if I succeed, His blessing will be for me alone. If I sin against Him, that's my responsibility too, and I'll bear the punishment or the results. So don't bother me. Keep your nose out of my business!" But that's not possible. John Donne wrote, "No man is an island, entire in itself." If I sin against God, I hurt you, for "we are members one of another" (Eph. 4:25, KJV). The results that come to my life have inevitable impact on you, for we are one body in Christ. Can you imagine smashing your thumb with a hammer and your ear saying, "Boy, I'll bet that hurts, doesn't it? But you'll get over it soon." Not a chance. The entire you is hurting and the entire you is jumping up and down, shouting, "Yow!" or some other suitable phrase. If one member of a fellowship is really experiencing God's blessing, the whole group is uplifted. And if one member is out of fellowship with God, inevitably that has an effect on the entire membership.

We see this over and over again. As we are out of fellowship with God, the results go all through society, in terms of how we live with one another, how we see one another. When we are out of fellowship with God, how much easier it is to look upon another person as an object for our own gratification. When out of fellowship with God, how much easier it is to say, "Well, I worked for my money. Let him do the same. Forget him." When out of fellowship with God, how much easier it is to think, "The system's ripping me off, so I have a right to rip off the system." We destroy each other when we slip away from a commitment of ourselves to God.

The Old Testament prophets frequently came back to this issue. "Why is it the poor are downtrodden?" they asked. And answering their own question, they cried, "Because you are out of fellowship with God. If you were in fellowship with God, experiencing His unconditional commitment, His passionate loyalty to you, you couldn't help but have that same commitment to others. If His love was pouring into you, it would have to pour out. But because it isn't pouring in, you use people!''

Can you hear one of the crowd saying, ''Wait a minute, Isaiah or Amos or Jeremiah, I've never used anybody!'' Now see the prophet pushing through the throng to that man, laying his hands on his shoulders and looking deeply at him, his own eyes filled with blazing compassion, ''But Zeke, have you never looked the other way when someone was being used? How dwells the love of God in you?'' The only answer is a bowed head.

We are part of one another. Whether we think so or not, our commitments to God are not lived out in isolation. I owe it to you to keep faith with God and you owe it to me. Our lives are in each other's hands. Handle gently, please.

Breaking Faith

Now in what way were the Judeans breaking faith with one another? ''Abomination has been committed in Israel and in Jerusalem'' (Mal. 2:11, RSV). *Abomination* is as strong a word in Hebrew as it is in English. It means something horrible, detestable, almost too awful to be named. In a very general way, it is attached to practices which are abhorrent to life as God created it.

But what is this terrible thing? ''Judah has profaned the sanctuary of the Lord which He loves and has married the daughter of a foreign god'' (v. 11). Many Jews were marrying outside the covenant. This was one more symptom of their growing absorption into the society of the day. But they said, ''So what? The golden age of the Messiah has not come. We are not the rulers of the world. Who knows what's happening? There's obviously no reason for us to be as snooty about our distinctives, as we have been in the past. If we see these lovely pagan girls, why shouldn't we marry them, particularly if they are rich? What is the difference?''

Malachi's answer, ''It makes all the difference in the world. Breaking faith at this point has an impact upon our whole society. You bring paganism right in among us. You're profaning the sanctuary of God.''

Those who believe that Malachi was still addressing the priests in this paragraph point to his reference to the sanctuary as evidence. That may be so, but I wonder if we do not have here a forerunner of the New Testament concept of the temple. What is the sanctuary of God? His people. So when Paul heard that the Corinthians were dividing into a "Paul" faction, a "Peter" faction, an "Apollo" faction, he cried out, "Don't you see what you are doing? You are breaking up the temple of God. It's as if you took an ax to the temple to chop it to pieces. Don't you realize that you, the fellowship of believers, are the sanctuary of God?" (See 1 Cor. 3:16-17.) Malachi was saying the same thing, "You have brought paganism right into the sanctuary, the fellowship, by doing this."

How many times we deceive ourselves. A Christian marries a non-Christian and says, "Well, I'll lead him to the Lord." Perhaps because there are fewer sharp Christian men than women of that caliber, and because a woman usually waits for a man to propose marriage, there seems to be a somewhat higher proportion of women in this predicament. Over and over again you see a lovely Christian girl marrying a non-Christian, and saying, "It's all right. I'll lead him to the Lord." When you meet that girl years later, she is struggling to bring up her children as Christians, for her husband will have nothing to do with Christianity. Then she says, "Oh, I made a terrible mistake."

The believer and unbeliever are of different families. The one is a child of God. The other is a child of someone else, a "foreign" god. That difference is manifested in their approach to life. Because a person doesn't care to commit himself or herself to Christ, that doesn't make him a monster or a Satan-worshiper. In fact, some of the nicest people we meet are unbelievers. But it finally comes down to two radically different approaches to life. One says, "Let's commit this situation to God and trust Him to bring us through His way." The other says, "Are you crazy? 'God' helps those who help themselves!" To the unbeliever, the thought of surrendering control of his life, his future, and security into the hands of the Unknown is incomprehensible. So Malachi warned, "You have enough problems already without marrying a pagan." Weeds grow naturally enough in a garden without the gardener deliberately scattering seed that will grow into misery.

Church Discipline

You have a stake in whom I marry, as I do in your choice. Something about that really makes our American individualism bristle, doesn't it? "Hold it, buddy, I'll marry whom I like and you can keep your nose out, thank you." Where is that commitment to each other, that willingness to submit my wants and desires to the scrutiny of my brothers and sisters? Where is that submissiveness to the best interests of the community? Where is that willingness to look not only to my "own interests, but also to the interests of others?" (Phil. 2:4, RSV) "Be subject to one another out of reverence for Christ" (Eph. 5:21, RSV).

But that can sometimes get sticky. What if we disregard our brothers' and sisters' love and wisdom and proceed down a road which pretty clearly leads from selflessness to selfishness? The Prophet's words are like a thunderclap: "May the Lord cut off from the tents of Jacob, for the man who does this, any to witness or answer, or to bring an offering to the Lord of Hosts" (Mal. 2:12, RSV). Ezra, Nehemiah, and Malachi were faced with that ugliest of problems: discipline. The Scriptures are painfully clear. We are responsible to correct and admonish one another in love. If we will not, it is because we do not love enough. Because we want to avoid pain, upset, and trouble, even at the cost of leaving a cancer untreated in the body.

Obviously, there is a vast difference between "telling off" and admonishing. Interestingly enough, we do the former more easily than the latter. Get a cozy little discussion going about the color of the new carpet or whether the chancel ought to be open or closed, and we'll "tell off" anybody and everybody. But let a brother or sister start becoming emotionally involved with someone other than their spouse—a situation which has every unbeliever in town in stitches—and we only make an inner judgment. We act as if everything is normal, and we leave the two parties and the fellowship to drift down Niagara toward the falls.

In thinking about discipline, the question always arises: "Do you believe the church is a club for saints or a hospital for sinners?" That is called the "either-or" fallacy of logic. Neither one is the truth, for there are more options than these two. The church is never to be a halo-polishing society. It is more like a lifesaving station. But if one member can't row, and two are bickering about who's in charge, and three don't know where the water is, leaving only one who can do the job, the church is really nothing. And I fear there are a lot of "nothings" masquerading as churches. This is so because we have not been clear in our objectives, and have not been committed enough to each other to point out to one another where we are missing the mark. And paganism, not nastiness or meanness but plain old untrusting self-will, pours into the body like fog into a valley.

Now obviously you do not take a big society church, as nice as vanilla pudding and as pagan as the devil, and throw all the bums out. What do you do? John Wesley faced the same problem in 1740—a great state church, comfortable in its beautiful ritual, ostensibly orthodox, and yet dead. So what did he do? He organized. As someone said, "He organized to beat the devil." That's exactly right. He formed small groups of disciplined people who had some glimpse of the eternal city and were willing to be apprised of every weight that kept them from getting there. Those people cared about each other. They prayed with each other, rejoiced with each other, agonized with each other, and leveled with each other. Anybody who began to drift was admonished and exhorted, but if he continued away in the face of all that, he was removed from the roll. The seas were too steep, the night was too dark, the stakes too high to have an oarsman in the boat rowing backwards.

The upshot was that they reformed the Anglican Church. It was not without a split, of course. But the many thousands who stayed in the state church brought it new life.

Where are those disciplined core groups today? Where are people who care enough about the honor and glory of God, the welfare of the body of Christ and the life of their brothers and sisters to *commit* themselves to one another? Where is God? He is in the midst of the churches, walking with those who care and conquer (Rev. 3:4-5).

10
DID YOU MARRY FOREVER?

Another thing you do: You flood the Lord's altar with tears. You weep and wail because He no longer pays attention to your offerings or accepts them with pleasure from your hands. You ask, "Why?" It is because the Lord is acting as the witness between you and the wife of your youth, because you have broken faith with her, though she is your partner, the wife of your marriage covenant.

Has not the Lord made them one? In flesh and spirit they are His. And why one? Because He was seeking godly offspring. So guard yourself in your spirit, and do not break faith with the wife of your youth.

"I hate divorce," says the Lord God of Israel, "and I hate a man's covering himself with violence as well as with his garment," says the Lord Almighty.

So guard yourself in your spirit, and do not break faith.

Malachi 2:13-16

Two broken covenants. And now a third. The priests were corrupt in their search for their own glory. The people had abandoned one another in their concern to gratify their own desires. And now what about the home? As Malachi narrowed his focus yet again, the heartrending truth emerged that there was no commitment in the home either.

Not only had the men broken faith with the community by marrying pagan girls, but they had broken their covenants with their first wives to do it!

Divorce Is a Tragedy

It is not my desire to place any divorced person under increased guilt. Malachi is very clear on the issue of divorce and I want to be equally clear. Divorce is not an acceptable way of handling marital problems. But through Christ we may know the forgiving grace of God. If you are divorced, the past may be truly put behind you in Christ and you may set out on the road ahead with a sense of forgiveness and grace. Do not beat yourself for what is gone, nor plaster over any wounds you still bear. Day by day, offer yourself to Him for what you are, infinitely precious, and receive His healing grace. Although God hates divorce for what it does to people and society, He loves divorced persons. You are not condemned to be forever looked upon as a failure in God's eyes. Christ died that you might not be viewed that way. Instead, God sees you as His son, His daughter, in whom potential for growing and loving is limited only by your capacity to receive.

Sometimes, as we have tried to express God's sovereignty, we have conceived of Him as having a master plan of history where all the moves are worked out in advance. Then when we make a botch of things and clearly miss some move, we wonder if we are not forever-more doomed to second-best. Perhaps a truer picture of God's sovereignty is that of the Master Weaver who works His apprentices' mistakes into the overall design in such a way that the outcome is all the more beautiful. That is real sovereignty. That is the work of a God who makes even the wrath of men praise Him (Ps. 76:10). The dissolution of your marriage was a tragedy. But even out of that tragedy the sovereign God can bring blessing, if you will allow Him to do so.

Marriage Is Forever

But this confidence is no reason for those of us who are still married, or yet to marry, to look at the relationship with crossed fingers: "Well, if it gets rough, I can always bail out." No we can't, not as far as God is concerned. In marriage, as in no other human relationship, the truths of faithfulness, commitment, and selfless love are lived out. From that point of view there can never be another like your first husband or wife.

Why? Because marriage is forever. It is a covenant. One might argue that *covenant* and *contract* are synonymous. But in the biblical context, they aren't. A contract is an agreement between two parties in which they agree to provide stated services, often for a stated length of time. But they do not give themselves unconditionally. In the biblical sense, a covenant is unconditional self-giving, for that is what God has done. He has given Himself to us.

Today marriage contracts are becoming popular. "I will provide certain services and accept certain obligations, but do not ask me for myself." Such people refuse to commit themselves. They reserve the right to themselves for themselves.

But Jesus' words come across the centuries, "Whoever wants to save his life will lose it" (Luke 9:24). Self-identity is like a bubble; grasp it for yourself and it disappears.

We define ourselves in relationships. Who am I? For one thing, I am the husband of this woman. I am the father of these children. But there are no genuine relationships without commitment. And that is why marriages based on contracts are doomed from the beginning. Apart from that trust which grows out of the total commitment of ourselves to one another, we are not going to open ourselves to each other in ways that make a lasting relationship possible. And thus, we are never going to find ourselves.

One of the factors in the present situation is our nearly total misconception of love. It is perhaps too easy to blame the entertainment industry for this problem; but they are at least the most visible contributors. For us in America, love is a "squishy" feeling in the pit of the stomach. You know the story: "Some Enchanted Evening" she or he walks in the room, and boom, it hits us and we're IN LOVE. Love is thought to be an attraction—fatal or otherwise. So in all earnestness, we go before the Parsons Brown of the world and pledge our undying LOVE to each other. But curlers and a mudpack are very hard on squishy feelings, as are a two-day growth of beard and a shirt which stands up in the corner by itself. Even harder are the discoveries that he has the most incredible habits or that her idiosyncracies you used to think were cute are maddening after a month of total exposure to them. What to do? "Well, we don't love each other any more, so it's all over." Or, "Actually, we haven't loved each other for years. And I really saw that when I met this young woman in the office. We were so right for each other, etc. This being so, we would really be false to ourselves if we went on living a lie." Or would they? Is it a lie?

Love, in the biblical sense, is not a feeling. It is an act of the will. You see, feelings can't be commanded. They flit through the consciousness like birds through a forest. They can be adapted, adjusted to, directed, but they pretty much come and go as they will. But the will can be commanded. And so the Bible commands us to love.

But what is it we're commanded to do? The basic idea of love is choosing. Did you get that? Choosing to say, "I love you" is to say, "I choose you. Out of all the people in the world, I choose you with whom to share my life, with whom to rear children and commit to them the traditions and secrets that make life worth living. I choose you when you're sick. I choose you when you're grumpy. I choose you when you're old. I CHOOSE YOU."

Do you remember the feeling you had as a child when sides were being chosen for some game? Maybe it was Red Rover. You were in the pool of those to be chosen. And your best friend was one of the two captains. Remember how it felt when he chose you first, even though you weren't the biggest or the fastest? You jumped out of the pack and ran and stood with your captain, alone together for all the world to see. It was the greatest feeling in the world. Chosen!

On the other hand, do you remember the feeling when that "best friend" chose somebody else first and then somebody else and somebody else? You had lead in your stomach and you didn't care if you played another game of anything, ever. You were rejected.

I don't normally think of Barbra Streisand as one of our great contemporary theologians, but she sings a song which says it all. It asks, "Why Did I Choose You?" and concludes, "If I had to choose again, I would still choose you." That is love. And you and I can offer that to someone, the most precious gift in the world. Now don't misunderstand me. I am all for squishy feelings! How good of God to make our biology so that the process of finding and uniting with a mate should be accompanied by such a glorious array of feelings. But that's not love. Choosing someone because they make me feel good may be the most selfish and unloving action in the world. Only when I choose what will build you up and enhance you and make you more confident of your worth, *regardless* of my feelings, can I truly say I love you.

So marriage is forever. And as the initial tempest of feelings subsides, a couple can begin to learn the true pain and exaltation of consciously choosing each other in every circumstance of life. That's not the time to quit, but to begin! The couple that learns how to do this is a walking exhibit of what it is to deny themselves daily. But they are also a walking exhibit of the fact that the burden is light. It may seem that they must simply grit their teeth and pay the price of utter self-surrender for the sake of their mate, without any sense of God's presence at all. And that feeling may go on for days or months, as they doggedly force their wills to do what they must for the sake of God and their mate. But, as Elizabeth Goudge, a British author, says, "The mystery plays fair." The day comes for this couple when they discover Someone is carrying them and the burden, and feelings of tenderness, delight and joy which they may have given up ever knowing again come tripping over themselves to fawn on this husband and wife.

This picture is seen so clearly in Proverbs where the phrase "the wife of your youth" appears. The writer is pointing out the folly of going after an adventuress, but it could be equally well said, an adventurer.

> Drink water from your own cistern,
>> running water from your own well.
> Should your springs overflow in the streets,
>> your streams of water in the public squares?
> Let them be yours alone,
>> never to be shared with strangers.
> May your fountain be blessed,
>> and may you rejoice in the wife of your youth.
> A loving doe, a graceful deer—

May her breasts satisfy you always,
  May you ever be captivated by her love.
Why be captivated, my son, by an adulteress?
Why embrace the bosom of another man's wife?

(Prov. 5:15–20)

Love as a feeling is not to be found in the embrace of adventurer or adventuress. It is found in the arms of that first mate whom we have chosen in all our youthful naivete and enthusiasm, and for whom we have learned to pay the last price of self-denial to choose again and again. When we determine to stop looking elsewhere for gratification and instead give ourselves to gratifying, we will begin to discover what real satisfaction is.

A woman dreamed she was in hell. To her amazement she saw great banqueting tables loaded with every kind of food. This certainly was not like the hell she had heard about. Then she saw it. The diners, who were seated on either side of the table had their hands fastened immovably upon their eating utensils, and those utensils were three feet long. So she watched with growing horror as the diners struggled to feed themselves. One would aim his spearlike fork at a choice piece of roast beef, and others, seeing his choice, would scramble to get it first. Finally, someone would emerge triumphant from the melee, meat impaled on his fork. But there was no way to get it in his mouth; the fork was too long. All up and down the tables, this was taking place. Cries and snarls of frustration and anguish filled the air.

Then the dreamer was transported to heaven. To her utter astonishment she saw the same situation: the great tables groaning under every imaginable kind of delicacy; the diners seated on either side of the tables; the impossibly long eating utensils fastened in every hand. She wanted to cry out, "But this isn't heaven!" And then she saw that the people were feeding each other, across the tables! All too often, the difference between heaven and hell is not the situation but ourselves.

Marriage *is* forever. In that lifelong commitment, knowing we have been chosen irrevocably, we can learn what it is to let down our defenses, stop grabbing, and start giving. We can learn the true meaning of love and begin to demonstrate that to a lovesick world.

Marriage Is Completion

But marriage is forever because of the very nature of the bond. Man and woman were made for each other. Each is incomplete without the other, and having once been put together, they do not come apart without violence. The Book of Genesis provides the background. God said a very curious thing about Adam: "It is not good for the man to be alone" (2:18).

The repeated refrain in the first chapter of Genesis was, "And God saw that it was good." Bible scholars have remarked that these are the words of an artist. An artist has an idea and begins to translate that idea into pigment on canvas. Being human he can never make a perfect translation, but if he's a good artist he can come close. So one day he will stand back and say, "That's good," meaning, "Yes, that's the way I envisioned it." Now do you see what God was saying after each phase of Creation? "That's good; that's what I dreamed of, planned for. It's just right."

But then He said, "This is *not* good." What did He mean? He meant Adam was not humanity as He dreamed of it. This male was not complete and would not be until he found himself in the female component of humanity and until she found herself in the male component. So it is neither accident nor mere biological attraction that boys and girls fill each other's attention during the teen years. They do not need mere animal fulfillment. They need that which is bone of their bone, flesh of their flesh. They need to find completeness in each other.

And what happens when they do? "Therefore shall a man leave father and mother, and shall cleave unto his wife; and they shall be one flesh" (Gen. 2:24, KJV). No longer are they two individuals; now they have become one person. Of course, the becoming one flesh has a sexual reference, and a beautiful one. Our bodies are made for each other, for an expression of our incompleteness apart from each other. But the context makes it clear that much more than physical unity is involved here. Up to the point of marriage, a man defines his identity by reference to his parents. But after that point it is defined by reference to his wife.

This is not a submerging of the wife's identity into the husband's. It is the mingling of two formerly separate identities into one new one.

No longer *"my* car," *"your* house," *"my* money," *"your* job." Now it is *our* car, *our* house, *our* money, *our* job. It is, as the popular song says, "The two of us against the world." That is the beauty of the Old English word *cleave*. We are called to "hang on to each other for dear life."

There are forces in the world which hate the achievement of truth they see in the mingling of female and male into one person. And those forces will drive an insidious wedge between spouses wherever they can. Have you ever been to a party and watched husbands and wives pick at each other? The husband tells a story and all the while the wife is making catty remarks. The wife gives her opinion on some political issue and the husband blurts out, "That's dumb. What do you know about it?"

Remember the Hebrew word *hesed*? *Hesed* is that passionate loyalty which *refuses* to think the worst about our covenant partner and always chooses the best. I have always loved Karen for this in her. She is passionately, sometimes a little embarrassingly, on my side. Oh, how I have needed that, because it has made me more and more secure in her love and God's, and thus a better person. She has corrected me many times, but always quietly and rarely publicly. And I am trying to learn to be just as loyal to her. For our own sakes, we cling to one another, not selfishly or possessively, but because we have found ourselves in each other. Anything which deprives my wife of me will cripple her, and anything which deprives me of her will cripple me. We have become one flesh, and God is a witness to that fact.

Divorce Is an Act of Violence

But someone says, "Well, that's all very nice if you have a good marriage and have really become one flesh in a spiritual as well as a physical sense. But our marriage was a wreck from the beginning. The thought of us being mutually dependent on each other is a laugh. We're like two cats whose tails have been tied together and then hung over a clothesline. We're destroying each other by our very inability to get free of each other."

I'm sure that is the case in some situations and I don't want to bomb anyone with oversimplifications. But most cases are not anywhere near that desperate, at least not in their formative stages. And the fact is that whether we have tried or not tried, whether our mate was "right" or "wrong" for us, we have in a real sense become one new person in God's eyes. To break up any marriage, even a bad one, is to promote a death. And despite God's forgiveness and healing, divorced persons will have a part of themselves missing. They can never go back to being the individuals they were before. Something of themselves has been given away, not to be gotten back.

This is why God says, "I hate divorce." He rejects it as a way of dealing with our marital problems. He rejects it as an open option for us to consider at any moment along the way. Why? Because it constitutes violence. When I first saw those words in Malachi, I wondered why divorce should be considered an act of violence. Surely the whole thing *could* be handled on a very adult, understanding basis. But the more I thought about it, the more I saw the truth of the biblical statement. Divorce is the rending of a relationship where deep sharing has bonded two selves together in ways which can only be broken by force.

This is seen so clearly in the lives of many of the proponents of "open marriage." They thought that two adults could share a relationship in which total loyalty to each other was an unnecessary possessiveness. They would be open with each other about their liaisons with other lovers, but both would know their primary commitment was to each other. Today many of these couples are divorced. God just did not make us that way. The jealousy which wants the lover for oneself alone is largely a manifestation of a God-given expectation, the expectation that there is one to whom I can give myself without reserve and in whom I can find myself forever.

But divorce is violent not only because of the rending of the personality bond. It is also a manifestation of a violent attitude. What is a violent attitude? It is the attitude of the world: he who takes gets. The only way to get what you want is to take it. Most of us don't physically strike people in living out this attitude. We're too refined for that. But we have been taught that happiness is ours by right, and that happiness can be achieved by manipulating people and situations to do our bidding. Therefore, we have the right to manipulate people and situations. Robert J. Ringer's book, *Winning Through Intimida-*

tion at first had to be published privately because no publisher would take it, thinking it a little too brash for society's taste. In other words, it's OK to use people as long as you don't talk about it. When the book began to sell in the thousands, the publishers saw the light and rushed to get out similar volumes. Of course, we have violence in the streets. We are imbibing it at the fountainheads of our civilization! So when a man complains to his wife, ''I have a right to my happiness and you aren't giving it,'' or a woman accuses her husband, ''You are stifling my fulfillment as a person,'' they are both saying. ''I must take what I want.'' That is violence.

I'm glad Malachi speaks to the men here, because all too often it is the wife who is blamed for a divorce. And many women who bear relatively little blame for the breakup of their homes nonetheless berate themselves for their failure. Don't do it! It was that overblown masculine ego that was to blame. Here Malachi is describing our own times to a T. More and more marriages are collapsing in their third decade. Why? Because the men are in their 40s by that time. They're on the downhill side of life. They're not going to rise much higher in their professions. The adventures that were going to happen ''next year'' haven't happened. So there comes that subtle temptation to prove to oneself, ''I'm just as young as I ever was.''

And along comes a fluffy-headed 18-year-old who ''adores mature men.'' Suddenly the ''wife of his youth,'' that 45-year-old woman at home, looks pretty haggard and rundown. She's just borne his kids and kept his house and washed his dishes for 23 years. Who wouldn't look 45? She has given him the beauty of her youth and the loveliness of her trust through the years when he was nothing. And now, at the point where she most needs the security of his love, she is pitched out on the junk heap.

A man with whom I once worked told of saying to his wife, ''Mamma, your fenders are getting pretty dented up. I believe I'll trade you in on a new model.'' She said, ''Just remember, big boy, they don't make the new models like they did these old ones.'' Exactly. There will never be another model like the wife or the husband of your youth.

In the ancient world, all that was necessary for a man to divorce his wife was for him to say three times, ''I hate (or reject) you.'' But God says, "*I* hate (or reject) *that*! I reject divorce as a way of meeting your needs." Why? Because the problem is not "out there." It's "in here." If we are unhappy in one situation, we are likely to be in another. Most divorced persons, having known what it was to be one with someone else, even in a bad "situation," are very lonely being single. But what happens when they succumb to the loneliness and remarry? Bad news. Do you know one reason why the divorce rate is now calculated at two out of five? Because so many of the second and third marriages are coming apart. People take the causes for their unhappiness with them when they desert one marriage and head into another.

We do not achieve a sense of personality integration and well-being through the manipulation of persons and situations. It is ours when, having come to the end of our resources and abilities, we throw ourselves into the arms of the heavenly Father and allow Him to give what we've been trying to take, allow Him to supply what we've been trying to manufacture. Happiness? Maybe yes, maybe no. But that is in His hands to give. Serenity, yes. Power, yes. Freedom, yes. The consciousness that our spouse no longer has the power to destroy us, and that we now have the power to reach out to our mate in redemptive love.

Godly Offspring

But there is another reason why God rejects divorce as a means of supplying our needs. The children. This is expressed in Malachi 2:15. Now the first part of this verse is very difficult. It isn't that we don't know the words—we just don't know how they go together, that's all! Look at these various translations:

And did He not make one? Yet had he the residue of the spirit. And wherefore one? (KJV)

Has not the one God made and sustained for us the spirit of life? (RSV)

Did not the one God make her, both flesh and spirit? (NEB)

Did He not create a single being that has flesh and the breath of life? (JB)

But not one has done so who has a remnant of the Spirit. And what did that one do? (NASB)

Has not [the Lord] made them one? In flesh and spirit they are his. And why one? (NIV)

You were united to your wife by the Lord. In God's wise plan, when you were married, the two of you became one person in His sight. (LB)

It would be hard to find that wide a divergence for any other passage in the Bible. Who is the "one"? God, Eve, the wife, marriage? No one knows for certain.

Be that as it may, the second part of the verse is very clear. What does God desire? Godly offspring. And we ought not let the uncertainties concerning the first part prevent us from admitting the truth of the second. As Mark Twain said, "It's not the parts of the Bible I don't understand that bother me; it's the parts I do understand."

One of the functions of marriage is to make it possible for the children to be like God. But divorce makes that difficult. Why? There are at least three reasons. The first is the need for *security*. In his poem "Death of a Hired Hand" Robert Frost defined home as "the place where, when you have to go there, they have to take you in." Home is the place where some things are sure, in a very unsure world. It may be a very imperfect home. Dad may holler a little too much and Mom may gripe some. But it's fixed, almost like the sun and the moon, and a person can bank on it.

One of the loveliest pictures of this is the mother hen and her chick. The chick, a little ball of fluff, goes pecking his way off into the wide world. Not a care in that world. But suddenly it raises its head and everything is strange. With a horrified peep it whirls around and there is mother, her wings outstretched. Like a yellow streak, the chick scuttles across the barnyard and under that wing which clamps down around him. A few moments later, out pops the little yellow head, and from that position, he is ready to take on the world.

That's what the home should be—a place of certainty from which a child can go venturing off into the world and, when he needs to, come scuttling back to. But often, we parents are so intent upon building our own security that we have not time to provide our children with such a base. "I have a right to be happy, and if I'm happy, the kids will be happy." What we conveniently forget is that for Dad to leave Mommy, or vice versa, is to make a child's world fall apart. What was accepted as sure and without question has broken. The capacity to ever again accept anything at face value is deeply wounded. Also it is known that the majority of children from broken homes blame themselves for the break. It will be very difficult for that child to again be secure in his world or in himself.

Secondly, the home is where a child learns his *identity*. Benjamin DeMott, writing in the November, 1976 *Atlantic*, explored family life after the sexual revolution and suggested that whatever forms family and home take in the coming years, the one thing we must have is the capacity to convey to our children their own past and traditions. If we lose that, he said, we have lost ourselves, our children, and our future. So a boy learns what a man is, and a girl learns what a woman is, by reference to the man and the woman who form the focal points of their lives. That man and woman show the boy and girl the distillation of 40 centuries of civilization on this planet. And if they are wise parents, they allow the children to find themselves against the backdrop of that tradition. Parents who act as if they can ignore the understandings which have grown up across those centuries, are misguided, at the least. Those who think a girl can be reared without her dad or a boy without his mom have missed the lessons of history and wish disaster on us all by sending rootless, formless infant/adults out to possess tomorrow.

There is yet a third reason why the home is the key to children becoming godly people. And this is the most important of all. The first two are preparatory. A secular home where a man and a woman are comfortable in their own traditions and roles can produce mature, understanding offspring. But such homes cannot produce godly offspring.

So it is that the home is God's *theological seminary*. Here is where those basic biblical truths are taught. It is not enough merely to convey a sense of one's past to a child, important as that is. More important is the necessity to convey the biblical traditions. Deuteronomy 6 is so poignantly clear on this.

Hear, O Israel: The Lord our God, the Lord is one. Love the Lord your God with all your heart and with all your soul and with all your strength. These commandments that I give you today are to be upon your hearts. Impress them on your children. Talk about them when you sit at home and when you get up. Tie them as symbols on your hands and bind them on your foreheads. Write them on the door frames of your houses and on your gates. . . .

In the future, when your son asks you, ''What is the meaning of the stipulations, decrees, and laws the Lord our God has commanded you?'' Tell him, ''We were slaves of Pharaoh in Egypt; but the Lord brought us out'' (6:4-9, 20-21).

The truth and character of God are to be so much an intrinsic part of the parents' life, and so much a part of the content of their conversation with the child, that the child will come naturally to that place of inquiring what God has done to implant these so deeply in the parents' lives. Then the great historic acts of God, culminating in the redemptive work of Jesus, can be shared and explained, not merely as Bible stories, but as revelation, and they can become a part of the child's basic rootage.

But what is the truth and character of God? And how are they conveyed in the family? Where else can a child learn the strong fatherly love of God than in the home? Where else can a child learn the tender motherly love of God? Where else can a child learn God's complete acceptance of us, even when disapproving certain of our acts? Where else can a child learn the meaning and practice of unselfish commitment? Where else can a child learn that God is utterly faithful and can be depended on completely? However poorly a given home may communicate these values, there is no other place they may be learned as well. And even if the home is not overtly Christian, if there is any measure of integrity, love, and responsibility, the child will have gained the appropriate framework into which God can reveal Himself in coming years.

The Faithfulness of God

Above everything else is the concept of faithfulness. As we discussed earlier in this book, the major factor God had to overcome in revealing Himself to human beings was their belief that He could not be trusted. A vicious circle was in operation then and it still operates today. Knowing humanity to be untrustworthy, we see God in the same way. But if God is untrustworthy, should we be overly concerned about faithfulness? Using people, using God—the gods—that's the name of the game. So it went, and so it goes, around and around.

How to break that circle? Not by God beating us over the head and saying, "You bums! Start being more faithful to one another or I'll smash you!" No, He bound Himself to a man and a woman first. "Abraham, Sarah, I'll give you the land, the child, the future you want. I promise." They dared to trust Him, and wonder of wonders, He kept His promise! He was faithful! Then He bound Himself to the Hebrew people. And again He kept His promises. Slowly the Hebrew people got the picture. "Well, if it is really true that the Creator of this world is faithful, we'd better be too. We'd better forsake the old selfish independence which is destroying us and discover what it is to commit ourselves to others and to Him."

Not only was the old circle broken, but a new one was put in its place. Believing God to be trustworthy and faithful, they sought to be also. And as they manifested a new faithfulness, others began to say, "Well, God must be the way they are." That's why God says that the person who swears to his own hurt may dwell with God (Ps. 15:4). The person who keeps his word even when it doesn't work to his own advantage is the person who truly demonstrates the faithful character of God.

What is your marriage teaching your children about the character of God? Is it teaching them that they have their needs supplied if they are committed to themselves? Or is it teaching them that He who sits at the heart of the universe will supply all their needs, that He longs to do so if they will only entrust themselves into His hands? Is it teaching them that love is a feeling? Or is it teaching them that love is commitment, faithfully performed in the midst of joy and sorrow, affection and anger, communion and alienation, hope and despair?

"Where are You, God? I cry to You. I weep for You before the altar of my emptiness. I groan after You by the long ascents of my loneliness. Where are You?"

And across the windy darkness comes a small, quiet voice: "You have driven Me from the sanctuary by your refusal to commit yourself to your calling, your people, your own family. You have called Me to your festivals, paraded your offerings before Me. You have sung 'All to Jesus I Surrender,' yet have never given up your own glory, your own rights, your own will in the concrete affairs of life.

" 'If you are offering your gift at the altar, and there remember that your brother has something against you' (Matt. 5:23). Learn the meaning of commitment to your brothers and sisters. Then your emptiness will be met with fullness and your loneliness with homecoming.''

11
IS GOD TO BLAME
FOR YOUR TROUBLES?

You have wearied the Lord with your words.
"How have we wearied Him?" you ask.
By saying, "All who do evil are good in the eyes of the Lord, and
He is pleased with them," or "Where is the God of justice?"
Malachi 2:17

Why hadn't the people of Israel made a wholehearted commitment to God? We have looked at three reasons.

● The priests had not committed their glory and prestige to God for the sake of the people.

● The people had not committed their personal rights to one another for the good of the group.

● Married persons had not committed themselves and their happiness to their spouses.

The result of all of this was a deep sense of malaise and social instability, and the feeling that somehow God was responsible for their troubles. He was not keeping His side of the bargain. God simply was not just.

At first it may sound strange that they blamed God. Yet this has been a pattern through the ages. We cry the loudest about injustice when we have lost the power to commit ourselves to something or Someone higher than ourselves and when all our covenants are in ruins.

This tendency is illustrated by a study done at the federal narcotics hospital in Lexington, Kentucky. Two groups, one composed of professional persons with no drug history, and the other composed of addicts, were asked, "If I offered you $500 today, or $5,000 in six months, which would you take?" Almost without exception the nonaddicts chose the $5,000, whereas 85 percent of the addicts chose the $500. When asked why they would take the lesser amount, most answered something like, "Well, I'd have the money today. And anyway, you probably wouldn't keep your promise."

These addicts were from a segment of society which says, "Get it now. Indulge yourself. You go around only once. Life will rip you off if you're not careful."

What's the Use?

But why does commitment to self and to immediate desires leave one with a conviction that God is not just? Let's look again at the road down which the Judeans have walked.

● They served God in order to be blessed. But this is using God. It says, in effect, that God exists for us, to serve our purposes. It promotes service without commitment. It bargains as Jacob did, "If You bless me, You can be my God." There are times when God will play along with that game, but not for long. Sooner or later, the Eternal, the Ineffable will meet us and lay down the gauntlet—all or nothing. The Judeans had been to that point. With their mouths they said, "All." With their lives they said, "Nothing."

● They weren't blessed. God will not be manipulated. He wants to pour out spiritual and material abundance upon us, but He can't until we come to that humiliating point of saying, "God, I cannot make you give Your gifts; I cannot deserve Your gifts; I can only receive them." Like the Judeans, we want to tell ourselves that God has blessed *us* because of the particularly sterling nature of *our* theology, or *our* worship, or *our* church government. All the time we are oblivious to the quiet background noise—God vomiting.

● They served Him poorly. They said, "What's the use? We don't get anything out of it." Their worship deteriorated. Why give the best if you're not going to get a return? The quality of their lives deteriorated. Convinced they could not trust God to supply their longings, they became increasingly grasping and selfish. Transient and ephemeral humans, they longed for glory. Physical beings, they longed for goods. Spiritual beings, they longed for love. They could not understand that the more they longed after these, the farther they moved from them.

● They concluded it didn't pay to serve God. "Look," they said, "if you really want God to bless you, be a crook. It's apparent that the thugs are the ones God really likes." The crooks not only prospered; they could spit in God's face, taunt Him, and still go scot-free. Famous atheist Robert Ingersoll used to offer to prove God did not exist. He would call God every vile name he could think of, and degrade His honor. Finally Ingersoll would dare God to strike him dead—if He was a God who cared about the honor of His name. Ingersoll ended every such outburst triumphantly alive. That would have impressed the Judeans.

One might ask why they served God at all? Because, like us, they lacked nerve. Probably there is a god out there and if so, he is likely big enough to get us if we were to ignore him completely. So although we can't figure out how he operates, we'll keep on giving him something just to keep him on our side. We seldom stop to think how inexpressibly sick and tired God must be of all this garbage. When Malachi let the people in on this startling little secret, they were quite shocked and offended. "We wearied God? How?"

Is God Unjust?

When we are trying to use God to achieve our purposes, when we will not submit our desires to Him, it is only natural that we should think Him unjust. We try to make our ways His ways, and the result is always disappointment. But what happens when we seek to make His ways ours? When we say, "I want Your way for me"? The change in attitude is dramatic.

The Prophet Habakkuk asked many of the same questions as the Judeans of Malachi's day. Like them, he looked at promises apparently unkept, at injustices seemingly unpunished, and cried out, "Art Thou not from everlasting, O Lord my God, my Holy One?" (Hab. 1:12, KJV) "Where are You?" he seemed to be asking. The answer he received was the bold announcement that righteousness *will* reign.

The announcement was followed by a stunning vision of the coming One. In other words, his question was answered with another promise.

This emphasis is similar to Malachi's. But the responses are completely different. As we have seen, the Judeans responded with cynicism, "Come on, God, we'll believe that when we see it. In the meantime we've got our lives to live. Get out of the way." How different was Habakkuk's answer!

"Though the fig tree should not blossom,
And there be no fruit on the vines,
Though the yield of the olive should fail,
and the fields produce no food,
Though the flock should be cut off from the fold
and there be no cattle in the stalls,
yet I will exult in the Lord,
I will rejoice in the God of my salvation.
The Lord God is my strength,
and has made my feet like hinds' feet,
And makes me walk on my high places" (Hab. 3:17-19, NASB).

One of my colleagues has said, "I can just see Habakkuk sitting out there in a barren field on a dead mule, praising the Lord." None of Jacob's spiritual blackmail—if You bless me, I'll serve You. If You get me out of this mess, I'll do what You want. Habakkuk had come to that place where he could allow God to be God. He was committed, come what might. Habakkuk had learned enough of God's love in past days to trust Him now. He had walked closely enough with Him on balmy summer days to be able to discern His hand in wintry storms. Instead of manipulating God, he consigned himself to God. Because he had discovered who could fill the empty place in his soul, everything else could come or go, if he could just have Him. Blessed is the man who knows what he wants.

The Judeans did not understand that belonging to God was what they wanted. So they accused God of injustice in not giving them their inordinate and selfish desires. But that accusation is loaded with irony. Did they, of all people, really want God to be just? Justice starts at home and those who have the most light will receive the most searching judgment. How little they understood God's justice. If God were truly just, they would be the first ones destroyed. But they could not see how their craven selfishness, their casual heartlessness, their strutting pride cried out to God for separation and punishment. All they saw was God's apparent unfairness in regard to their petty desires.

Do we want immediate and impartial application of God's justice to all persons right now? Not if we know ourselves, we don't! In fact, when we cry to God for justice, we usually want a strictly partial justice, one that will work in our behalf. Isn't it amazing that when someone wrongs us, we cry for justice; but when we wrong them, we want mercy!

God's Dependability

Though the Judeans did not understand the magnitude of the question they were asking, God did. For the universe is a mirror of God's consistency. As in the natural realm, so in the moral realm, certain actions must eventually bring certain results. God's utter dependability is key to our understanding of the world. We plan our lives around the consistency of the physical universe. If I live in Iowa, I do not expect to open my front door one day and find the Indian Ocean or the Alps in the front yard. If God were to arbitrarily suspend the results of certain actions, the whole universe could come apart. He *must* be just.

So what to do? How could God keep His covenant promises and still be just? God had promised in covenant to make the descendants of Abraham more than the sands of the seashore or the stars of the sky and to bless the whole world through them. But now their failure to keep their own covenant demanded their destruction.

Someone had to die, but who? Micah asked this question.

> With what shall I come to the LORD,
>   and bow myself before the God on high?
> Shall I come to Him with burnt offerings,
>   with yearling calves?
> Does the LORD take delight in thousands of rams,
>   in ten thousand rivers of oil?
> Shall I present my first-born for my rebellious acts,
>   the fruit of my body for the sin of my soul?

> He has told you, O man, what is good;
>   and what does the LORD require of you
> but to do justice, to love kindness,
>   and to walk humbly with your God? (Micah 6:6-8, NASB)

Killing rams or children could not efface the effects of the people's resistance to justice, kindness, or humility. Only a human being who had never sinned could die for one who had. Only God in human form could die for all. Only of Him could it justly be said, "Upon Him was the chastisement that made us whole" (Isa. 53:5, RSV).

But the Jews were not the only ones in a covenant of death. The entire human race was under such a bondage. Death, both physical and spiritual, has come upon us all. Physically, this death came through Adam and Eve. Because they became mortal, we their children are also. But there is a worse death than the physical one. The spiritual death of alienation from God goes on forever. This is what Adam and Eve began to experience as soon as they sinned. We do not inherit spiritual death from them, but we do inherit from them a predisposition to disobey God, to deny His godhead over us. When we follow out that predisposition, as all of us do, we die spiritually. Like the Hebrews, we too are under the curse.

Some solution had to be found for the death—the spiritual separation from God—of all mankind. Humans could not solve the problem. The dead could not revive the dead. It was up to God to defeat our enemies—and His—by Himself. Perhaps in the process of that defeat, He could turn His people from Judeans into Habakkuks.

Perhaps He can convince us, against the backdrop of His utter faithfulness, of the folly of our religious attainments. Perhaps in the light of His complete commitment we will become as nauseated as He is with our half-hearted religiosity. Perhaps if we see God taking all the injustices of the world upon Himself, we may be able to let down our self-made barriers against pain and loss, and entrust ourselves to the Father's hands.

Oh God, I am so tired of all this, and I know You are too. I can't make it. Is it really true that You have come? Let it be so for me. Let the reality of Your presence melt my apathy. Give me the will to be completely Yours.

IV
THE SON
OF GOD

12
WHY IS YOUR GOD ON A CROSS?

"See, I will send My messenger, who will prepare the way before Me. Then suddenly the Lord you are seeking will come to His temple; the messenger of the covenant, whom you desire, will come," says the Lord Almighty.

"But who can endure the day of His coming? Who can stand when He appears? For He will be like a refiner's fire or a launderer's soap."

Malachi 3:1-2

"Herein is love, not that we loved God, but that He loved us and sent His Son to be the propitiation for our sins" (1 John 4:10. KJV). God's love for you and me can never be more clearly communicated than in His coming into the world. He did not stand off and shout instructions. He came to us and bore our griefs and our sorrows. This is the only answer to our cries for justice and satisfaction. For in Jesus, evil is punished and righteousness triumphs. He is the proof that God is just.

A vast, seemingly endless crowd stood on a great plain. Without being told, they somehow knew that this was the last judgment. But the judgment throne was empty, and as they waited, the crowd grew restless. Finally from somewhere out of the mass, a voice cried, "How can God judge me? He doesn't know what it is like to be a member of an oppressed minority—to be hounded, and driven, and crushed. How dare He judge me for my hatred?"

There was a moment of silence at such audacity, but then another voice took up the cry. "That's right," it said. "God doesn't understand what it's like to live in poverty, not knowing where the next meal is coming from. How can He judge me?"

Then like a flood came the other voices: "Yes, how can He judge a refugee?" "Or someone who's been tortured?" "Or those who have been robbed of justice?" Finally, as with one voice, the whole throng shouted, "God, You can't judge us. You can't say we did wrong in our situations, because You were never there."

Then slowly, beginning at the front of the crowd, the cry died away. For there, ascending the throne was not some divine caesar, but the Man of Galilee. The One on whom God laid the iniquity of us all (Isa. 53:6, KJV). He has walked where all of us have, yet without sin. Jesus is the answer to the problems of injustice in the world— the answer the Prophet Malachi held out to his own people and to us.

The One Awaited

But wait. Was Malachi really talking about Jesus? Or was he only saying in a general way that God Himself would deal with the world's problems? That he does indeed have the Messiah in mind can be seen in his grasp of the essential facts of Jesus' life and ministry. These include the preparatory ministry of John the Baptist, Jesus' deity, and His relation to the covenant.

Notice that there are two messengers mentioned here. The first one will prepare the way for the second who is the messenger of the covenant, the Lord coming to His temple.

This is exactly how it happened. After Malachi, the Lord sent no more prophets for 400 years. To a nation which had become accustomed to at least one prophet per generation, this absence was shocking. Then after 400 years of silence came the word that there was a prophet preaching and baptizing in the wilderness of the Jordan. It's no wonder that the Gospels tell us "all Jerusalem and Judea" went out to hear him.

And what was this prophet's message? It was distinctly preparatory. He talked about repentance and baptism because the One who would come after him was going to bring in the kingdom of God. And once Jesus was well-established, John was content to drift into obscurity.

As if this circumstantial evidence were not enough, Jesus specifically identified John the Baptist as being the person Malachi spoke of.
Jesus asked the people why they went out to see John. To see a
prophet? "Yes, I tell you, and more than a prophet. This is the one
about whom it is written, 'I will send My messenger ahead of You,
who will prepare the way before You' . . . . And if you are willing
to accept it, he is the Elijah who was to come" (Matt. 11:9-10, 14,
NASB).

Jesus not only quoted Malachi 3:1, but further confirmed Malachi's
prophecy by quoting Malachi 4:5, where the prophet compared this
preparatory messenger to Elijah. It is clear that Jesus thought Malachi
was speaking about Himself and John the Baptist.

Sender and Messenger

The second piece of evidence that Jesus alone is the coming One who
is God's answer to the world's cries for justice is in the duty of the
messenger. Notice that Malachi speaks of one who is both the Lord
and a messenger of the Lord's covenant.

How can a person be the sender and the messenger? The two are
mutually exclusive. He is either sender or messenger, he cannot be
both. But Jesus can. He is the Son of God! According to Malachi, the
messenger who is to come is divine, yet represents a God who is
beyond Him. That is exactly what Jesus did. He is God through and
through, yet He is not the Father. So at one and the same time, Jesus is
the Lord, and also the messenger of the Lord and of the Lord's
covenant. Malachi could not have represented Jesus' unique character
in a better way.

In fact, only as Malachi foreshadows Him and the New Testament
represents Him could Jesus be the answer to our cries for justice. Only
if He were fully human and fully God could He embody the message
we need.

What do we need? We need to be able to know God, and also to
know that we are at peace with Him. That's what the covenant is
about. And that's why Malachi called Him the messenger of the
covenant. In the first place, Jesus does what the covenant was designed to do—He shows us the face of God. Looking at Jesus, we

know who God is. Paul says, "He is the image of the invisible God" (Col. 1:15). In other words, if we could take a picture of the space where God is, it would be Jesus' face which would appear on the developed film.

But who could endure that face? The Jews thought the messenger of the covenant would be a great leader who would destroy their enemies and make them rulers of the world. It is small wonder they had difficulties with Isaiah 53. They reacted just as Peter did: "Jesus, You're not going to die on some cross. You're going to rule the world and we're going to help You!" (See Mark 8:32-33.) Their Aramaic paraphrase of Isaiah 53 claimed that it was their enemies who would be bruised and whipped by the Servant of the Lord. They could not believe that *they* were the enemies for whom the Servant must suffer. Walt Kelly's "Pogo" was exactly right when he said, "We have met the enemy and they is us!"

That is what the covenant had shown the Hebrews across the years. Gathered there around Mt. Sinai, the Hebrews saw no particular problem in serving God perfectly. Of course, they would obey His commandments and experience His kingdom. Nor did the tragic experiences of the wilderness and conquest years seem to teach them much about their own spiritual stubbornness and blindness. On the eve of his death, Joshua had to warn them about the naive enthusiasm they were showing about keeping the covenant.

Slowly across the years they began to realize that the covenant was a mixed blessing. On the one hand, it was a source of delight (Mal. 3:1), showing them God's way of living—indeed, the very face of God worked out in human life. How proud they were to be the sole possessors of God's Torah, or instruction. On the other hand, it was a source of despair. A good Jew was speaking in Romans 7. The closer he adhered to the law, the more it destroyed him. The more he said, "This is the way I'm going to live," the more it became clear he couldn't live that way. The people of the covenant could not do what they had sworn to do.

And being unable to defeat their spiritual foes, they were then unable to defeat their physical foes. So they cried out, "Who will deliver us from this double bondage—bondage to our enemies, yes, but more than that, bondage to our sins?" This theme appears in all the great prophets: Isaiah, Ezekiel, Jeremiah. "We cannot deliver ourselves. We have tried, and only sink deeper into the mire." The answer that comes with greater and greater insistence is: "I will."

Isaiah, troubled by the folly of arrogant, unprincipled leaders and the unrepentant spirit of the masses, saw the mighty arm of the Lord revealed in the coming kingdom of the Child where, through His own servanthood, righteousness and justice will reign (Isa. 9:1-7; 11:1-9; 51:9; 52:10; 53:1).

Ezekiel, grieved by the stony hearts of his people, saw the day when God would act to put a new heart, a heart of flesh, of obedience, within them (Ezek. 36:25-32).

Jeremiah, seeing the old covenant with its condemnation driving his people deeper and deeper into despair, excitedly proclaimed the day when God would operate from within, bringing forgiveness and hope (Jer. 31:31-34).

So as the Old Testament era drew toward its close, the people were rising on tiptoe, crying to the watchmen, "Do you see Him? Has He won the victory over our sin and bondage?" The answer was yes. "Listen! Your watchmen lift up their voices; together they shout for joy. When the Lord returns to Zion, they will see it with their own eyes" (Isa. 52:8).

When Jesus did come, He perfectly embodied this two-edged nature of the covenant. For, on the one hand, He showed them all they were meant to be, but weren't. It is no wonder the Jews could not endure Him. Suppose there were a mirror in my room which showed me all my sins and shortcomings each time I looked in it. What would I do with such a mirror? Right! I would smash it. We want a mirror that shows us how good we look.

But Jesus was a fully realistic mirror to the Jewish people. They had said, "Well, we may not keep the law perfectly, but we're doing all right." Then Jesus came along to be the mirror of their souls. He showed them, by contrast, who they really were, and it was too much for them. Messenger of the covenant? "Away with Him! Crucify Him!" And their cry is ours.

The Sacrificial Lamb

But the covenant is not only curse; it is also blessing, the promise of

God's presence and care. And it is that side of the covenant which gives Jesus' ministry its primary meaning. How can God turn the curse into blessing? Who can turn the cry for death into the promise of life? Since we cannot do it, the Lord must. Isaiah pictured Him as a warrior coming up from Edom, the symbol of all that is in opposition to God. The blood of His enemies stains His garments.

> Why is Your apparel red,
>> and Your garments like the one who treads in the
>>> wine press?
> "I have trodden the wine trough alone.
>> and from the peoples there was no man with Me;
> I also trod them in My anger,
>> and trampled them in My wrath;
> and their lifeblood is sprinkled on My garments,
>> and I stained all My raiment.
> For the day of vengeance was in my heart,
>> and My year of redemption has come.
> I looked, and there was no one to help,
>> and I was astonished and there was no one to uphold;
> so My own arm brought salvation to Me;
>> and My wrath upheld Me" (Isa. 63:2-5, NASB).

But as Jesus hangs on the Cross—comes up from Edom—whose blood stains His garments? That of His enemies, like you and me? No. That of His enemies, like sin and sorrow, hatred and hell? No. It is His own. His own precious blood has become the blood of God's enemies.

"For He made Him to be sin for us, who knew no sin" (2 Cor. 5:21, KJV). Is God just? Oh, yes. Will sin be punished? Oh, yes. In fact, in Christ it already has been and its pangs need never be suffered by anyone.

Jesus has become the sacrificial Lamb which satisfies the covenant and secures our Passover. Can you imagine what went through the minds of the disciples that night in the Upper Room, when Jesus held up the cup and said, "This is My blood of the covenant"? Their minds must have instantly traveled back across the centuries to that day when Moses, having read the law and heard the people's shouted assent, lifted up the basin and cried, "Behold, the blood of the covenant!''

But what did Jesus mean? In the succeeding days it became clear. Jesus' blood shed on that cross forever satisfied the old covenant. It put to silence that blood oath which cried out against them. In the Jewish idiom it paid—gave *shalom* or peace—to the unpaid debt.

But Jesus was not merely the messenger of the old covenant's satisfaction, He was also the sacrificial Lamb who made possible the ratification of a new covenant between us and God. "For this reason Christ is the mediator of a new covenant, that those who are called may receive the promised eternal inheritance" (Heb. 9:15). This is the fulfillment of what Jeremiah longed for: a new covenant written on their hearts, a knowledge of God which would take root within, a new confidence of sonship which would promote obedience. And that ratifying blood, according to the writer of the Book of Hebrews, speaks more graciously and insistently than the blood of Abel (Heb. 12:24). Abel's blood, like the blood of the slain bulls, cried out for vengeance. Jesus' blood cries out for forgiveness.

> Five bleeding wounds He bears,
> Received at Calvary;
> They pour effectual prayers,
> They freely plead for me.
> "Forgive him, oh forgive," they cry,
> Nor let that ransomed sinner die.
>
> Charles Wesley

This then, was God's answer to the problem of justice. The Hebrews cried, and many of us have joined them, "Where is the God of justice? Why do the wicked prosper and the righteous suffer?" They might also have asked, but being human they didn't, "What *will* You do with the problem of evil, God, both ours and theirs? You can't just ignore it all. But neither can You instantly balance every account in this terribly interlocked world."

With devastating simplicity, the answer comes: Jesus. Where is the God of Justice? On the cross. The cross stands out like a lightning rod on the highest hill of time, drawing to itself all the hurt, the agony, the tragedy, the anguish of this broken world. There our sordid little dramas are played out, our haughty dreams paraded, our brutal duplicities unveiled.

Does God know our struggles? Yes. Does He care? Yes. Is He just? Yes. As God's blood oozes and later gushes down His body, and down the stem of the cross—that grim plant reared by human pride— we know He is just. No sin goes unpunished, no horror forgotten, by the Man on the cross.

13
CAN YOU STAND BEFORE GOD?

He will sit as a refiner and purifier of silver; He will purify the Levites and refine them like gold and silver. Then the Lord will have men who will bring offerings in righteousness, and the offerings of Judah and Jerusalem will be acceptable to the Lord, as in days gone by, as in former years.

Malachi 3:3-4

Imagine a scene like this: A husband has been blatantly unfaithful to his wife. Now he comes back, sorry and repentant for the shame and grief he has caused her. He begs for forgiveness, and somewhere she finds reserves of love and warmth from which to summon that forgiveness. But one thing she won't say is, "You can go back now to your lovers and your affairs. I've forgiven you and that's all that matters."

Forgiveness assumes a turning away from the past and commitment to a new kind of life. To be sure, forgiveness is not purchased by turning away from the old life, but neither does forgiveness ignore behavior. Forgiveness wipes the past clean so that a new relationship can be entered into.

That's why the message of the coming One has two sides. On the one hand He tells us that the cause of justice will be served; that sin will be borne, and loss and anguish shared. It tells us, on the other hand, that sin will not triumph. Its roots will be attacked at the same time that its effects are being experienced.

It is not enough that our sins should be forgiven. God made us for fellowship with Himself, and something must be done for us so that we will not repeat the sins which drove us from Him in the first place.

Again Malachi foreshadowed a significant part of Jesus' ministry, in his specific prophecy of the Messiah. He said that the Lord would suddenly come to His temple. Jesus did not come simply to erase the past. He came also to take up residence for the future. This is what John is speaking about when he called believers to abide in Christ. As Christians, we have the privilege of making Christ at home in our hearts.

Since the beginning of time, God has intended to share His presence with people. The tragedy of the Fall is that Adam and Eve were excluded from God's presence. And God was as heartbroken over that state of affairs as they were. He immediately began to make plans for His homecoming to the human heart, to share His presence with His children.

Tabernacle and Temple

The Book of Exodus helps us to see that this sharing of Himself is God's ultimate purpose with us. The climax of the book is not the Red Sea Crossing nor the giving of the law. Those are a means to an end. That end is seen in this: "And the glory of the Lord filled the tabernacle" (Ex. 40:34). God brought His people out of Egypt, and revealed His moral and ethical nature to them, so that He might live in their midst.

The amount of space given to describing the tabernacle gives us an idea how important it was to God to be with His people. Twelve chapters of Exodus are given to that description: seven in the future tense, telling how the work should be done (25—31); and five in the past tense, telling how it was done (35—39). Clearly the tabernacle, the place of the Presence, was of special significance.

Ezekiel did something similar when he devoted the last nine chapters of his book (40—48) to a highly detailed description of a new temple in Jerusalem. Solomon's temple had replaced the tabernacle. Now the Babylonians had destroyed that temple and carried the people into exile. Would God ever live in their presence again?

Ezekiel's answer was that they would be restored to their land and that God's glory would be seen in them.

Some believe that Ezekiel's temple will be built in the millennial age, but it is also possible that the prophet gave all those careful instructions to demonstrate the importance of God dwelling in our midst. For surely, the true temple of God is the human heart. He will never be content merely to dwell among us. He means to live in us.

That, according to Malachi, is one of the reasons Christ came. He came as the Lord to His temple. The new covenant is one of grace, grace to forgive from past sins and the grace of His presence to provide a dynamic for the bearing of fruit in the future.

So the answer to our questions about God's justice is found in Jesus. Yes, sin will be punished. In fact, it already has been, our offenses as well as those which have been done to us. But will righteousness prevail? Again in Jesus, the answer is yes. The empty tomb is a witness. For when evil had done its worst against the best Person who ever lived, He broke its bars and rose in His righteousness to live out His life within His people.

The Holy Spirit

But how does Christ live in us? How does He purify and refine us? When John the Baptist foretold of Christ, he gave us the key. "I baptize you with water for repentance. But after me will come one who . . . will baptize you with the Holy Spirit and with fire" (Matt. 3:11). There it is. Jesus will come to His temple to refine it and purify it through the Holy Spirit. In fact, John spoke as if that was the main point of Jesus' coming.

This idea that God's Spirit would be the means of God's love, faithfulness, and righteousness becoming real in people was not new with John. The Hebrew people had observed across the years what happened when people became wholly committed to God: They began to show the same spirit that could be seen in God. There was new boldness and confidence. Often special skills came to light. There was a new readiness for service. There was an effectiveness to their lives which had not been there before. And above all there was a new moral sensitivity. They could see the implications of a given decision or action, as it related to God's revealed will. They had a new passion for justice, for truth, indeed, for God and for man.

There was a growing awareness that only as people were actually lived in by God could they really be what God wanted them to be, and even more, what *they* wanted to be. Thus, some of the great promises of the prophets fell upon fertile ground.

Thus says the Lord who made you and formed you from the womb, who will help you, Do not fear, O Jacob My servant; And you Jeshurun whom I have chosen. For I will pour out water on the thirsty land and streams on the dry ground; I will pour out My Spirit on your offspring, and My blessing on your descendants. . . . This one will say, "I am the Lord's;" and that one will call on the name of Jacob; and another will write on his hand, "Belonging to the Lord," and will name Israel's name with honor (Isa. 44:2-3, 5, NASB).

I will sprinkle clean water on you, and you will be clean; I will cleanse you from all your filthiness, and from all your idols. Moreover, I will give you a new heart and put a new spirit within you; and I will remove the heart of stone from your flesh and give you a heart of flesh. And I will put My Spirit within you and cause you to walk in My statutes, and you will be careful to observe My ordinances. And you will live in the land that I gave to your forefathers; So you will be My people, and I will be your God (Ezek. 36:25-28, NASB).

And it will come about after this that I will pour out My Spirit upon all mankind; And your sons and daughters will prophesy, your old men will dream dreams, your young men will see visions. And even on the male and female servants I will pour out My Spirit in those days (Joel 2:28-29, NASB).

These statements, and several others like them, promised that in the coming age, God by His Spirit would live in them and enable them to *be* His people. Not only would past sin be forgiven; there would be a new dynamic by which they need not continue in sin.

This was what Malachi was speaking of when he said that the

servant would *refine* and *purify*. What good is it to have the past forgiven, if there is no prospect of being different in the future? If the same impurities which messed up the past remain to mess up the future, what's the good of it all?

This was what John the Baptist was talking about. He was saying, "I can only offer you the blessed possibility of repentance and a new start. But He can offer that and more. He can offer forgiveness, plus a purging and an empowering which will make you new creatures." (See John 1.)

This is why Jesus said to His disciples, "If you love Me, you will keep My commandments. And I will ask the Father, and He will give you another Helper, that He may be with you forever; that is the Spirit of truth [or faithfulness]" (John 14:15-16, NASB). Having discovered what it is to be freely, totally forgiven, to be cherished with an endless love, we say, "Yes Jesus, we'll do anything for You." And Jesus, in His infinite wisdom says, "And I will send another, just like Myself, not only to stand with you but to be in you, enabling you to become what you want to be."

This is what the Resurrection is about. Because Christ lives today, He can abide in you and me. Just as we were dead in trespasses and sin, so Jesus was dead. And just as He conquered that death, so we may conquer trespasses and sin through His presence in us.

The Overcomer

How the devils of hell must have chortled that black Friday night. They had done their worst. They had torn the heart of God in two. They had killed the Prince—the One who was too just to let our sin go unpunished and too loving to let us bear it. How they must have danced around that prostrate body, chattering like demented squirrels in a frenzy of glee. They had won.

But no, they hadn't won. Evil often seems very brilliant, in the short run. But it never is, in the long run. They could not see the truth which is written on the universe: those who surrender eventually win. They could not see that by bearing the effects of sin, He "condemned sin in the flesh" (Rom. 8:3, NASB), and triumphed over it. They ought to have known. But they didn't hear the first strains of the song of the Lamb. Because He was slain, the Lamb earned the right to open the book of the destiny of all the living. "Worthy is the Lamb that was slain" (Rev. 5:12, NASB).

By taking the worst that death and hell could do to Him, by demonstrating what life is, in terms of voluntary self-denial for the sake of others, He broke the power of death forevermore. And He not only broke the death of the grave, but also the deadness which would operate in our daily lives. These days we see death all around us, its cold hand resting on our societal institutions. We feel its cynical breath wasting hope, trust, and innocence. But the word of the risen Jesus is, "Don't be afraid! I have overcome!"

I wonder what those dancing demons did on that golden morning when Jesus' corpse began to stir with life. Their gleeful chatterings must have died away in a moment. And what did they do when the Prince of the universe slowly sat up, an easy, confident smile on His face? They scattered to the ends of the universe, screaming the despairing cries of those who know they are beaten, who know they will be hounded until their destruction is final. "God has not given us the spirit of fear; but of power, and of love, and of a sound mind" (2 Tim. 1:7, KJV).

Live in Your Inheritance

But you may say, "Now, wait a minute. You were talking about the Holy Spirit in us, and now you're talking about the resurrected Christ in us. Which do you mean?" I mean both. Theologians may at times need to draw some distinctions between the two, but you and I don't have to. Jesus Christ, through the power of the Holy Spirit, longs to live in us and make us like Himself. The Holy Spirit of God, poured out on us, has one purpose: to manifest Jesus in us.

The big question is not whether you have a set of pat answers with which to split every theological hair. The question is: are you living in your inheritance? Is Christ's nature being worked out from within you? Or are you trying to work it in from outside you? The difference in those two is monumental. The one experience is delight; the other, drudgery. The one is trying to make a sailboat go by blowing on the sail; the other is feeling the surge as the wind of heaven fills the sail.

I do not want to mislead you. The person who is filled with God's Spirit is subject to emotional highs and lows. He is by no means immune to defeats, although these can be blessedly rare. Nor is "Christ in you" a cause to shut off your spiritual motor and coast. In some ways you will discipline yourself as you never have before; you will work as never before. But it will be discipline and work with a difference. Now the impetus will come from within, and though the work may be difficult and even tiresome, it will not be drudgery. And that's a big difference.

I travel a good deal and meet a lot of people. There is a startling contrast between Christians who have found the secret of Christ's resurrected life in them and those who have not. Of course, there are individual differences too, so that I have met jovial, energetic people who have found the secret and I have met some shy, introspective persons who have found it. Those who have not found are struggling, striving to attain. Those who have are relaxed, free, marveling in the wondrous things happening in them.

When I meet people who aren't living in their inheritance, I remember the story of a young man who was disinherited by his wealthy father. In a fit of anger his father had ordered him out of the house, shouting, "You'll never get a penny of my money!" The boy left, and nothing was heard from him for years. But on his deathbed, the father had a change of heart, and left all his millions to his son, instructing the family lawyer to find the boy. The lawyer traced the son through several ruinous episodes to his life as a bum. But there he lost the trail, and try as he might, he could not pick it up again. Totally frustrated, he finally gave up. The lawyer said, "Often my last thought before going to sleep is: somewhere tonight there is a bum, perhaps trying to sleep on a park bench, who is worth millions—if he only knew it."

You are no bum. Christ has done marvelous things for you and in you. However, if you are still struggling to be worthy of the forgiveness He has given you, you're not living in your inheritance. There is wealth already yours, if you will only claim it.

To claim that wealth, that abiding personal presence of Christ through the Holy Spirit, there is only one thing you need to do: give the temple completely to Him. He cannot fill what He does not possess. You may need to take two separate steps to make your gift complete. One is negative, the other positive. On the negative side, you cast out anything which is inconsistent with Christ's character, whether it be an occupation, a relationship, a hobby, a habit, or whatever. You may say with many of us, "But I can't!" Then let Christ do it for you. But *you* must do everything in your power to be rid of the offending behavior, if you are to experience His power.

On the positive side, you must be willing to follow out His will as it is revealed to you. Surrender which is unwilling to part with the unclean, and which is unavailable for the Master's use, is surrender in name only.

Refining and Purifying

All this helps us to see that the refining and purifying which accompany the presence of God are not a cosmetic treatment. They involve fire. When the burning coal touched Isaiah's lips, I don't think he said, "That felt so good! Do it again!" I think he cried.

If gold could weep, it would during the refining process, when the flame begins to play on the bottom of the crucible and the old familiar form with its comfortable assimilation of dross begins to melt. If pig iron could feel pain, surely it would cry out in agony as the flame is slowly but steadily turned up and up, and as the hammer blows fall on it harder and harder.

Is it worth the pain to be clean? Is it worth the fire to be pure? Is it worth the shaping to be tempered? Of course, it is. There is a delight and a satisfaction which nothing can produce at such a depth. But don't let anyone tell you it doesn't hurt.

When I was a teenager, the end of my thumb got in the way of a paper cutter. Only when the girl behind me gasped did I realize that an eighth of an inch of flesh and nail had been neatly guillotined. Some weeks later, an hour or so after our doctor had changed the dressing, I happened to lay the bandaged thumb on a stray sheet of paper. The bloody print it left told us there was a problem. When the doctor took off the bandage and examined the situation, he announced that a vein below the edge of the ragged nail was not closing as it should have, and would have to be burned shut with an electric needle. You can imagine my delight! Even with a shot of painkiller in the wound, the feeling of that electric charge searching under the nail again and again for the offending spot is one I'd rather forget. If faced with the same situation again, would I undergo that cure again? Sure. But not because it felt good!

The Lord comes to His temple in order to purify it. *Purity* is a word which has fallen on very hard times. *Pure* is something few teenagers would admit to. Part of the reason for this is found in the image we have succeeded in projecting to the world. *Pure* is a little old lady in a black dress, with a high collar and long sleeves. She has a flat black hat, a sweet smile, and a wicked umbrella. Of course, nobody wants to be put in that bag. Fear of being so caricatured has made many college women hesitate to admit they were virgins.

But that's not what *pure* is. *Pure* means "to be one thing." That gold which has been through the fire, and has had the dross skimmed off, is pure. It's not part this and part that, but all gold.

Earlier I said that to be at peace, or to have *shalom*, meant to "have it altogether," no loose ends, no embarrassing IOUs, no horses heading off in different directions. Well, in large measure, that's what *pure* means. Purity is to have your head on straight, and the debris of the past swept out. It means a clear understanding of what matters in life, of who matters in life. Purity is having a single motive: to please Him whom you love. When all is said and done, purity is integrity.

Without this purity, this singleness of heart and mind, it is very difficult to serve God. Only a clean cup can pour clean water. Only an unflawed wrench can stand up to the hardest strains. The Judeans had not learned this. Never fully committed to God, they sought to use Him and one another. Never knowing the freedom which comes from utter trust in Him, they always wondered whether they were getting as much as they deserved.

By contrast, the Apostle Paul had learned what it meant to be lived in by the risen Jesus. He knew that Jesus dwells only where He fills. For this reason, he was prepared to jettison anything which prevented that fullness, including his own personal pride and prerogatives. He was single-minded for God and His glory. Because He knew that God could be trusted, Paul could be free of self-absorption and care about others. He could be serenely content, in a palace or a jail cell. And he could rejoice in his own weakness. He had discovered what it meant to experience the fullness of Christ's ministry, for the Spirit had been poured out upon him.

Oh Lord, we want all of You. We want You to fill us with Yourself. Make us people of integrity. Set us free from the sin which would drive You from us. But Lord, sometimes we want all of You without giving You all of ourselves. Have mercy on us and by Your gentle, unwavering providence, bring us to that place where we know that what we hold on to, when we hold onto ourselves, is bitterness and despair.

14
DO YOU WANT PURITY?

"So I will come near to you for judgment. I will be quick to testify against sorcerers, adulterers, and perjurers, against those who defraud laborers of their wages, who oppress the widows and the fatherless, and deprive aliens of justice, but do not fear Me," *says the Lord Almighty.*

Malachi 3:5

The grocer in our little town says he can always tell when a genuine "revival of religion" is at work among us. People begin coming in to pay long overdue bills and to settle up for items they "borrowed" some time before!

What is he saying? That when our religion begins to get beneath the surface, it must affect our ethical behavior. This is why some observers of the contemporary scene are asking, "Where is the revival?" They ask this because students of religion see the late '60s and the '70s as a time of remarkable resurgence of the Christian faith. But so far we have looked in vain for the ethical renewal which has followed every other great revival. Some say that it is coming. We may devoutly pray for that. For without it, "the revival" will go the way of the hula-hoop and the trampoline center, as a fad with no more permanence than a soap bubble.

But why should vital faith in God always be coupled with ethical uprightness? Because of who He is! Of all the gods our world knows, the Christian God alone is characterized by ethical uprightness. All other gods are merely overblown projections of our human mis-shapenness. He alone stands over against us and shows us what we were meant to be.

This is what Malachi means in this fifth verse of the third chapter. The Messiah will not only be a messenger of God's forgiving love, or His abiding power. He will also be a messenger of God's ethical righteousness.

That message can be damning or it can be exhilarating. To the redeemed and Spirit-filled Christian, it is a message loaded with excitement. It says that I can be the person I dream of being. I can be like my Lord.

But to those who refuse to commit themselves to God because of pride, self-righteousness, lust, greed, or whatever sin, it is a message of damnation. He will either come as redeemer and purifier, or He will come as judge.

The Sorcerer's View

Malachi listed four particular sins here. While these might have been chosen merely at random, their significance and relation to each other make me believe that this selection in fact summarizes the whole catalog of ethical behavior. Each of these sins represents a whole class of sins, and each succeeding one grows out of the preceding. Let me explain why I see it that way.

The foundation of our ethical behavior is our attitude toward God. That is why sorcery is first on the list. The heart of magic is the attempt to manipulate God or the gods to make them do my will. It assumes that my wishes are paramount and that there are ways of making the social and physical forces of this world conform to those wishes. These ways are primarily physical and manipulative. *I* can make my world into my image. To be sure, in order to gain the supposed power, there may have to be the admission of greater power, but there is always the expectation of gaining dominance over the surrounding world.

This is the sorcerer's view. And it is a trap for many Americans who believe the ideas just expressed, but don't believe they follow sorcery. After all, they don't engage in those practices commonly called magical. What they don't realize is that the practices *follow* the belief. That they are the *result* of looking at the world in a magical way. Why do more and more Americans slip into openly magical practices? How can we hardheaded and skeptical people fall into the pit with horoscopes and mediums, wizards and spiritism? Because we have so long accepted the view that each of us can succeed by making our world conform to our wishes by using techniques which produce the desired effect.

During the history of America, those techniques have been materialistic. But now we are having to admit that they are failing us. For the forces which control the physical, psychological, and social worlds are not material but spiritual. Our pagan ancestors discovered this thousands of years ago, and in their wisdom, devised manipulative techniques to try to control those realms. We are following in their footsteps. But the sad truth is that those who attempt to control the powers of this world for their own purposes end up being slaves of the very powers they seek to exploit.

There are only two ways of looking at the world, and the gulf between them is immense. The biblical view is to recognize that the world is in the hands of a benevolent Father whom we cannot control, but who will give us what we want as we surrender control to Him and enter into His work—rather than trying to absorb Him into ours.

The sorcerer's way says that all that matters is contained *within* the observable universe, and that each of us is responsible for our own destiny. We can make the world serve us through the exercise of appropriate techniques.

One or the other of these two views must necessarily shape how we live, and how we treat the world and our fellow human beings. The person who takes the sorcerer's view, believing that it is paramount to achieve his or her desires, will take a very low view of faithfulness. That person will believe that honesty and integrity, particularly with someone else's reputation, are strictly relative to the results achieved. If it serves his purposes to be honest, he will. If it does not, he won't. In a similar way, he will look on those unable to defend themselves as merely things, to be used, benevolently, if possible, or ruthlessly, if necessary.

We can be thankful that many who take the sorcerer's view do not carry their position to its logical conclusion. But increasingly, as societal pressures intensify, we see those conclusions coming out. To see the ethical results of the path on which we are walking, we have only to look at pagan cultures.

On the other hand, the biblical view of the world leads, if rigorously followed out, in the exact opposite direction. How will the person who has committed himself to depend on a faithful God view marriage? Will he view it as a means of satisfying his own desires? And when those desires seem not to be gratified, will he deliberately cast his partner adrift? No, he will recognize in marriage a heaven-sent opportunity to learn the meaning of commitment, submission, and trust, an opportunity to discover new reliance on God for the meeting of needs, both individual and mutual.

How will the believer in the God of Jesus Christ view integrity toward a neighbor? Will he hold that person's reputation as a sacred trust? How can he do anything else, if he believes that God will supply every need, and that the supplying God never uses persons, but rather cherishes them?

How will the believer in the God of Abraham approach the weak and helpless? He will approach them as Abraham did Lot. If Abraham had insisted on the best land, Lot would have had to surrender it. But Abraham did not. For he knew that he could depend on God, and that he did not need to walk on people to get what was best for him.

A New Freedom

The teaching of Scripture, then, is that those who are the servants of God will be like Him, while those who serve Baal will be like him. The Lord who comes to His temple is faithful, unselfish, giving, and loving. Shall we receive His salvation and yet not expect to be like Him? We cannot make Him do our will. We can only receive the good He showers on us and the health He gives our spirits and in gratitude seek to be like Him.

To be sure, none of this is possible without the abiding presence of Christ. Unless He fills us with Himself, all of our striving for His likeness will be emptiness and frustration. But make no mistake. If He *does* fill us there will be a difference. There will be no toying with sin, no casual ungodliness, and no using of other people.

Perhaps you look at Malachi's list and say, "Gracious, I guess I haven't made it yet!" Cheer up, neither had Paul. He said that he had not yet attained perfection. Jesus was not done with him yet (Phil. 3:11). That's comforting to know, isn't it? But guess what else he said? That he had attained one kind of perfection which he urged on all his readers. That perfection is what we have been calling purity, and it has but one goal: to become all that Christ desires for us to be.

If we have allowed Christ to fill us and give us that single purpose for living, then our lives are going to be consumed with a passion to be like Him ethically. It is a lovely cycle, as by His spirit He begins to reproduce Himself in us. We find a new ability to care about others and to please the Father (Mal. 3:4). This achievement is so exciting we get thirsty for more Christlikeness. Each new satisfying drink increases our capacity. This cycle is not like the world's cycle, where each round higher diminishes our capacity for satisfaction. Here each round deeper only increases our satisfaction at being His, wholly His.

Make no mistake. If you have been filled with the Holy Spirit you have a new freedom, but it is not a freedom to live farther from Christ and feel less guilt. It is a freedom to live closer to Him, and to be more like Him than ever before, as you are being remade by His love. Anything else is a counterfeit.

Oh God, where are You? I see so much suffering and injustice in the world. Are You on the cross, carrying it all? Yes, I see You there. But Lord, I see so much emptiness and helplessness in myself. You know I love You.

Where are You? At the door of the tomb? In the fire and the wind? Yes, I see You there. But be no longer there, Lord. Be here. Be here.

V
THE TRIUMPH OF GOD

15
WHY DO YOU
ROB GOD?

"I the Lord do not change. So you, O descendants of Jacob, are not destroyed. Ever since the time of your forefathers you have turned away from My decrees and have not kept them. Return to Me, and I will return to you," says the Lord Almighty.

"But you ask, 'How are we to return?'

"Will a man rob God? Yet you rob Me.

"But you ask, 'How do we rob You?'

"In tithes and offerings. You are under a curse—the whole nation of you—because you are robbing Me. Bring the whole tithe into the storehouse, that there may be food in My house. Test me in this," says the Lord Almighty, "and see if I will not throw open the floodgates of heaven and pour out so much blessing that you will not have room enough for it. I will prevent pests from devouring your crops, and the vines in your fields will not cast their fruit," says the Lord Almighty. "Then all the nations will call you blessed, for yours will be a delightful land," says the Lord Almighty.

Malachi 3:6-12

Imagine you are a sincere though confused Judean who has just read the first part of Malachi's book. What has God shown you? By the very sending of His messenger Malachi, He has shown you that He does care about you, that He does hear your cry, and that He can do something about your situation.

Second, He has reminded you that He loves you and wants you to respond to His love.

Third, He has shown you that if you try to give Him cheap offerings and use Him for your own ends, you are demonstrating how little you think of Him.

Fourth, He has probed your way of life for an explanation of why you have been tempted to react to Him as you have. The answer, which is both cause and symptom, lies in your inability to commit yourself, either to God or to other persons.

All of this is brought to a head in the charge, "God is simply unjust. He does not reward the righteous nor punish the wicked. Why serve Him?"

God's answer to the charge was His promise to come Himself, in the form of the messenger of the covenant. Through that messenger justice would be done and people like yourself would be purified while those who persist in wickedness would be judged.

Try Me

What more was there for Malachi to say? In the final part of his book, he repeated many of the main themes and even duplicated the order of their presentation. But there is a difference. Now everything was said in the light of the promise of the Messiah. This makes the second part of the book even more relevant for Christians who have received the promise.

God seems to be saying through Malachi, "Can't you see that I am just, that I am trustworthy, that I am determined to bless the world? I am not insensitive to your cries. I will act decisively. So now let's look at these matters again."

In the light of His promises, God's cry to His people is: "Try Me! Give Me a chance to show you what I want to do for you. You have tried to make Me bless you, and it hasn't worked. You have tried to manipulate your lives without reference to Me and *that* hasn't worked. You've tried everything else. Now try Me."

That plea was not based only on the promise of the Messiah yet unfulfilled. It was founded also on the consistency of God which gave every reason to believe He would keep His promise and send the Messiah. "I the Lord do not change, O sons of Jacob; therefore you are not consumed.'' If God had been a changeable, arbitrary tyrant, Israel would have been burned up like a cinder long ago. He would not have put up with their stubbornness and their slowness to learn. But His unchanging desire was, is, and will be, to bless His creatures in every possible way.

The reference to Israel as Jacob's sons is so apt here, because God's determination to bless was nowhere more evident than in Jacob's life. With help from his mother, shrewd, selfish Jacob had worked himself into a box. He had decided to keep God's promises for himself. The result was not blessing but alienation and hatred. Yet, what a tough nut Jacob was. Perhaps only in his teens when he left home, he set out to live in a land he had never seen, to be with people he had never met, and the Scripture does not report even a flutter of nervousness. When night fell, he found a likely looking rock, propped his head on it and apparently dropped right off into the untroubled sleep of a baby. What a tough guy!

Yet there must have been the tiniest chink in his armor of self-assurance, because there was space for God to pour the light of His love and concern. God offered to bless Jacob in the same ways He had Abraham and Isaac. How did Jacob respond to that overwhelming offer? Did he fall to his knees in repentance and wonder? No. He said, ''Boy, this is a spooky place. I'll tell you what, God. *If* You keep your promises, I'll let You be my God and I'll give You back a tenth'' (see Gen. 28:16-22). *If!* Has God no pride? Why didn't He blast Jacob off the face of the earth? But when it comes to reaching people with His love, He truly has no pride. He will stoop as far as need be, even to death, to bless us.

This absolutely consistent desire to bless is what accounts for God's willingness to change. Yes, that's what I said: His consistency explains His changeability. The story of Jonah shows this. God had announced that Nineveh would be destroyed in 40 days. No ifs, ands, or buts. Yet when Nineveh repented, God changed His mind. Jonah got all over God for that. He said, ''I just knew You'd do that, God. I knew You were gracious and merciful, slow to anger, and abounding in steadfast love. I just knew You'd make a fool of me!'' A pagan god would have replied to Nineveh's repentance, ''I said I was going to destroy you, and I will. I don't care what you do.'' Not our God, He is so consistent in His desire to bless that if the conditions change in such a way as to permit it, He will change in a moment.

The Psalmist knew this, for he said,

> Sing praises to the LORD, you His godly ones
> and give thanks to His holy name.
> For His anger is but for a moment,
> and His favor is for a lifetime;
> Weeping may last for the night,
> but a shout of joy comes in the morning (Ps. 30:4-5, NASB).

Yes, God gets weary and angry with the games we humans try to play with Him. But He never *is* weariness; He never *is* anger. He gets weary; He becomes angry; but He *is* love. The one describes certain temporary reactions; the other tells us what He *is*, yesterday, today, and forever.

We see this exemplified in Jesus, as He thought about Jerusalem. When told that Herod was seeking to kill Him, He sarcastically responded that prophets were killed only in Jerusalem. But in a moment He slipped from sarcasm to heartbroken compassion.

> O Jerusalem, Jerusalem, the city that kills the prophets
> and stones those sent to her!
> How often I wanted to gather your children together,
> just as a hen gathers her brood under her wings,
> and you would not have it! (Luke 13:34, NASB)

Don't Rob Me

To the Judeans, God was saying, "Just turn around, repent, agree with my diagnosis, so I can be to you everything I want to be." But once again, their response boded ill. "Return to You? How? We never knew we had gone anywhere. Robbing You? Come on, God. How could we rob You?" Of course, the answer is by keeping what is rightfully God's.

How good God is! In the final analysis, everything is His. There are no completely self-made men. We did not choose our parentage. We had little control over the environmental circumstances which shaped us during our growing-up years. The amount of health and energy we enjoy is almost completely independent of our efforts—beyond a reasonable care to husband them and use them wisely. Unless we take our lives by our own hand, we know nothing of the place and hour of our death. All we are and have is God's! It was this truth which the rich fool of Jesus' parable would not admit. But it was so, whether he admitted it or not (Luke 12:16–21).

Now the lovely thing about God's treatment of the Jews was that He allowed them to spend 90 percent of His goods on themselves. He only asked that 10 percent be funneled into His service. You can hardly beat those terms. And yet the Hebrews begrudged them. Was it because they refused to admit whose money it was? You see, if this is *my* money which I produce, then I have the right to decide what I will do with it. And it is only rarely that I can ever "afford" to give anything to God.

On the other hand, suppose this is not my money. Suppose I hold it in trust. Then it is no longer my right to decide whether I can afford to give it. The question is whether I have a right to keep it, to divert to my use what is God's. Indeed, can I afford to *keep* it? For the good of my soul, I can't. Many who call themselves Christians have discovered to their sorrow that through their use of God's tenth, God has given them their requests, but has sent leanness to their souls (Ps. 106:15).

Why? Has God gone into a pout and said, "I'll fix you for that!"? No, but just as surely as there are physical laws in the universe, so there are spiritual laws. And to break those spiritual laws is to bring on ourselves certain results.

If you say to God, "I'm sorry, but I cannot trust You to supply my needs," conveniently forgetting that He has supplied everything you have, then there is no way you can receive the spiritual abundance He has stored up for you. If you say, "God, my love for You is not strong enough to make me want to give You the best, the cream, off my income," there is no way you can receive the wave after wave of His love.

Experience My Love

We experience this love only as we say, "Thank You, Lord, for the abundance which You have showered upon us. How can we show our delight in You? By giving back a measly tenth and enjoying all the rest? Why, of course! Here!'' Then we have broken down the barriers of selfishness, the walls of self-sufficiency, which prevented us from receiving all that God wants to pour upon us. Then we have put our trust into action.

Motives

There are several very dangerous ideas about tithing. Perhaps the most prevalent one these days is that we give in order to get. According to this idea, one has to ''prime the pump'' of God's abundance by tithing. Those of you who were raised around hand water pumps will know what I am talking about. These pumps depended on a leather suction ring to raise the water. But when the leather got dry, it curled away from the casing and no suction was created. So you had to pour a couple of quarts of water down the pump to moisten the ring before you could get back the several gallons you wanted.

That might be a good mechanical principle, but it is a very bad spiritual one. For it tempts us to say, ''OK God, I'll give this to You on the condition that I get it back with 900 percent interest.'' That's not a gift of love. It's an investment. Worse than that, it is an attempt to use God, which is exactly what the Judeans were doing. Love says, ''O Father, you've given me so much already. In Jesus You have given me a reason for living. And I know I can trust You to supply every need at just the right time. How can I give You enough?'' Greed says, ''I don't really think I can afford to give this. But if the odds are better than 50/50 I'll get it all back and more, I'll try it.''

A businessman heard his pastor offer to give back any tithes which had been paid over a year, if they had not produced tremendous blessings by the end of that year. Apparently feeling he had nothing to lose, the businessman started tithing. In the course of the year, he went bankrupt. So he asked for his tithe back! The minister, never having expected to back up his words in that way, did not produce. As a result the man brought suit against his pastor!

Why didn't God bless him? The way he reacted to the reverses of the year demonstrates that his attitude was wrong. He did not give a portion of his income out of love, or gratitude, or obedience. He gave in order to get. This businessman should not bear the blame alone. He had been encouraged in his attitude by a pastor who emphasized the wrong motive for giving.

When we give for the right reasons, every blessing, spiritual or material, will be viewed with delight because God doesn't *have* to do anything. But when we give to get, we feel that God is under obligation to us. With that attitude prevailing, hardly anything God could give would satisfy us.

The two brothers were twins, but they had radically different temperaments. One boy seemed incurably optimistic, while the other was terribly pessimistic. Their outlooks seemed so out of touch with reality that their parents finally took them to a psychiatrist. His decision was that they needed such an experience of reality as would lay a groundwork for further therapy. The little pessimist was put in a room with every kind of toy and game imaginable. The optimist was shut in a room full of horse manure. After a couple of hours the psychiatrist went back to check on them. He looked in on the pessimist first. He was sitting in the middle of the room crying at the top of his voice. "What's the matter?" the psychiatrist asked. "I'm just wondering when someone is going to come and take these all away from me," the child bawled. Shaking his head, the psychiatrist went down the hall to the optimist's room. As he got to the door, he heard cheerful whistling from inside. Opening the door, he saw that the boy had gotten a pitchfork from somewhere and was pitching manure from side to side. "What are you doing?" the psychiatrist asked. "Well," the boy relied, "with all this horse manure, there's just got to be a pony in here somewhere."

I suggest that those who give to get are a lot like the little pessimist: a whole room full of blessings could not convince them that God has kept His bargain. On the other hand, those who have experienced God's love and give out of response to that love are a great deal like the optimist: even in the horse manure of life they can find reason for gladness.

Material or Spiritual?

But this raises another question. *Does* God bless when we give out of sincere motives? In other words, *is* there a pony in here someplace? Some interpreters argue that we dare not carry the Old Testament promises of essentially material blessings over into the New Testament era. They point out, quite rightly, that the blessings which the New Testament promises in the Beatitudes, for instance, are primarily spiritual. These teachers claim that in Jesus' teachings, material riches were usually associated with spiritual insensitivity. Their argument is that God used material blessings as object lessons in Old Testament times to prepare for the understanding that spiritual blessings result from obedience to Christ.

There is a great deal of truth in this interpretation. Spiritual blessings are gifts of God which we must have. Too much of our own greedy gain is often attributed to God's blessing. For instance, it is highly unlikely that the wealth of Gulf and Western Corporation is the result of the direct blessing of God. And yet how easily we explain the financial success of a Christian institution or person as being a sign of God's blessing.

On the other hand, we dare not too easily separate the spiritual and material dimensions of life. As human beings we are both spiritual and material, and God does not neglect either side. Jesus makes it plain that we must attend to the spiritual considerations first. But He makes it equally plain that when we have done that, adequate material support will follow (Matt. 6:33).

History seems to bear this out. In those situations where the biblical ideal of life is lived out, there is a significantly higher level of material well-being. Wesley noted this with some regret in the case of his converts. Men and women who were formerly in the very dregs of society, squandering their beggarly incomes on liquor, gambling, and other pursuits, would come to Christ. The drinking and gambling would disappear. Because of their new honesty and sobriety they would be promoted to better paying jobs. They would begin to spend their money more wisely. As an inevitable result, their standard of living would go up. And, Wesley lamented, they were well on their way to becoming materialists!

Evangelist Luis Palau has said that if 70 percent of the adultery were wiped out in Latin America, 50 percent of the poverty would go as well. Since God has created the world by certain principles, then we *must* be better off materially as well as spiritually when we live in accord with those principles. The critical point comes when I as an individual brazenly go to God and say, "Because of my good behavior, You *must* bless me." That is not biblical faith; rather, it is heathenism. Biblical faith says, "Father, I deserve nothing from You, and if You will let me be a servant, I will love and honor You forever." Biblical faith says, "Though He slay me, yet will I trust Him." Biblical faith allows the sovereign Lord to dispose of us as He will, serene in the confidence that His plan for us is good. With that attitude, we can receive blessings He wants to give.

The Tenth and More

This consideration brings us to a final truth about giving to God. The tenth is not rigidly imposed on Christians as it was upon the Jews. It was rigidly imposed on them because it was an object lesson teaching spiritual truth. The spiritual truth is something like this: giving to God is a necessity for our spiritual well-being. As we make this physical surrender of our goods to God, we testify that all of our goods are from His bounty; we proclaim to the world that He is worth our best; and we affirm our helplessness to care for ourselves, and our trust in His willingness and ability to do so. Only in the light of these attitudes is it possible to have that living relationship with God on which our soul's life depends.

Now how did God go about getting the Hebrew people to realize these truths? He demanded that they give a specific amount, a tenth, of all income to Him. But how does this relate to Christians? Surely, giving is even more incumbent upon us now as a response to the gift of Christmas. But what about the amount? Here, those who live under grace must be very careful not to lapse into an external pharisaism.

How easy it is for us to say, "Well, I've given my tithe, so that's that." Or, "Oh dear, I gave only nine percent last month. God is going to get me. I'll have to hurry and make that up." This is not the spirit of freedom which Christ died to give us. John Wesley says it so well in his sermon, "The Use of Money":

Do not stint yourself . . . to this or that proportion. Render unto God, not a tenth, not a third, not half, but all that is God's, be it more or less; by employing all on yourself, your household, the household of faith, and all mankind, in such a manner, that you may give a good account of your stewardship . . . in such a manner that *whatever* you do may be 'a sacrifice of sweet smelling savour to God.'

Wesley is saying that a Christian must use *all* his or her money as coming from God. We cannot claim when we have given a tenth that God has no say about how we spend the rest. Nor, if we are handling all our money as belonging to God, need we be fearful if, at a given point, we are unable to give a tenth of our earnings directly into the Lord's service.

This makes life somewhat more complex. For now we cannot let an external demand settle the issue for us. It ought to provide the basis for our internal response to Christ, but it is only a basis, and in different cases that which Christ expects of us may differ.

For example, a family of four has an income of $250,000 a year and they let it be known that they are giving 50 percent to the Lord. The rest of us are suitably awed. Another family of six has an income of $7,500. They give only 5 percent. We look at one another out of the corners of our eyes and murmur that they would have a bigger income if they would just tithe. As a matter of fact, Jesus may be highly displeased that the first family is giving *only* 50 percent. Perhaps they could enjoy a very satisfactory standard of living and give 70 percent. On the other hand, He may be moved to tears by the sacrifice which the second family is making in scraping together a love offering of $375. You have to consider what they had left to live on. Even after giving 70 percent, the rich family would have $75,000 to the poor family's $7,125.

The question is not what can we *afford* to give. It is, what *ought* we to give as a sign of our love to God and our trust in His goodness. The tenth is an appropriate guideline and if we fall below it we ought to examine our consciences very carefully to be certain we are not simply deceiving ourselves about our giving. But we don't give because God will curse us if we give less than a tenth, or bless us if we give that much. Rather, we give because our hearts overflow with love and trust.

Testing God

Before we close this chapter we must talk about testing the Lord. We are told in Scripture that we are not to test God (Deut. 6:16). Jesus quoted this to Satan when he invited Jesus to prove God's love for Him by jumping off the temple (Matt. 4:7). Yet through Malachi God specifically invited testing. Is the Bible contradicting itself?

Some Bible teachers have suggested that the answer is in the difference between the words *test* and *tempt*, saying that it is all right to test God, but not to tempt Him. However, both *test* and *tempt* come from the same word. That word meant "to try something out, to see how fast it would go, how much it would hold, or how much it would stand." In one instance, it is wrong to see how far God will go. In the other instance, it is right. What's the difference?

The difference lies in the attitude which prompts the test. It is wrong to test God through disobedience or presumption. Because the Hebrew people did not trust God, they demanded proofs at every turn that He was God. If Jesus had succumbed to Satan's suggestion, it would have been the same kind of thing—"Before I enter this ministry, God, You're going to have to prove to Me I won't get hurt!" But Jesus trusted God too much to do that.

On the other hand, Jesus' whole ministry tested God, didn't it? Over and over, Jesus' obedience put God's faithfulness on the line, and over and over again God proved Himself. There is the difference. God delights when our obedience and love put Him to the test. Often, God's abilities have not been demonstrated in our lives because we have carefully kept ourselves out of situations where we might have to depend on Him. We have never let go of the strings of our lives long enough for Him to prove Himself.

Translated literally, "Be still and know that I am God" means, "Relax and find out that I am God" (Ps. 46:10). If we have never relaxed in His arms, we have not discovered what He can do in us. Then, when we run into a situation we can't handle, and when we feverishly rub Aladdin's lamp, only to find the genie out to lunch, we, like the Judeans, are deeply affronted. "Where are You, God?" we shout.

From somewhere very near, we hear a still, small voice: "I'm right here, right where I have been all along. It's just that you have never sufficiently committed yourself to Me in day-to-day obedience to be able to receive My power and abundance. And I cannot give it to you now, as much as I would like to, because the batteries of your receiver are dead. But they needn't be! Open up to Me in obedience and love, and find out what I can do!''

16
DO YOU
BELONG TO GOD?

"You have said harsh things against Me," says the Lord.

"Yet you ask, 'What have we said against You?'

"You have said, 'It is futile to serve God. What did we gain by carrying out His requirements and going about like mourners before the Lord Almighty? But now we call the arrogant blessed. Certainly the evildoers prosper, and even those who challenge God escape.' "

Then those who feared the Lord talked with each other, and the Lord listened and heard. A scroll of remembrance was written in His presence concerning those who feared the Lord and honored His name.

"They will be Mine," says the Lord Almighty, "in the day when I make up My treasured possession. I will spare them, just as in compassion a man spares his son who serves him. And you will again see the distinction between the righteous and the wicked, between those who serve God and those who do not."

Malachi 3:13-18

To answer God's renewed plea, some of the Judeans said exactly what they had before: "Why bother?" They couldn't see what good it did to serve God. Why go around with a religious face all the time, if you don't get something tangible out of the deal? If anything, their words have become even stronger. "Blessed are the proud and pushy." However, this hardening of their doubt is rather easy to understand.

For if we have begun to doubt God's love and justice, and then have heard His promises in Christ and His challenge to venture out in obedience and faith into the abundance of His grace, and refuse to do so, there is only one direction for us to go: toward increased doubt, increased bitterness, and ever increasing inability to see God's hand in life.

Amy and Mark

Amy Carmichael was a missionary to India. She gave her life to rescuing orphaned and abandoned girls. For these girls life would have held nothing except prostitution, abuse, and early death. Amy Carmichael brought them to a pleasant home, to a loving fellowship, and perhaps, most of all, to a life of dignity and worth. Yet Amy's health was marginal at best. She was often bedridden, almost completely so during the last 20 years of her life. She was often penniless. Talk about life dealing a bad hand! Yet her books breathe an air of gentle, joyous serenity. She had gotten a glimpse of the love of God in Christ which forevermore opened her eyes to what God was making available to her. In her book *His Thoughts Said, His Father Said*, she writes:

His thoughts said, "As I journey, sometimes the water is bitter."
His Father said, "Let My loving Spirit lead thee forth into the land of righteousness. Do not ask Him whether He will lead thee to Marah 'bitterness' or Elim 'sweetness.' Do not ask for the Elims of life. If thou must pass through Marah, fear not, for He will show thee a Tree, which, when thou shalt cast it into the waters, shall make the bitter waters sweet. One thought of Calvary will make any water sweet."

What a contrast to Mark Twain, whose story "The Mysterious Stranger" we mentioned in chapter 1. Toward the end of his life he was such a famous man that anything he wrote was immediately snapped up by a publisher. His lecture tours in America and Europe were sellouts. He was hugely wealthy. And yet, the older he grew the more cynical and depressed he became. He could discourse eloquently upon the stupidities and follies of human beings. The death of a beloved daughter only put the seal on his bitterness.

We cannot begrudge Twain his grief over the unexplained loss of his daughter. And yet, when one balances the books, it seems as if Amy Carmichael had more right to bitterness. Why did she not succumb, while Twain did? Surely, it is because she learned early to surrender her sorrows, her griefs, her disappointments into the hand of God whom she dared to believe loved her to the uttermost. Apparently Mark Twain, like some of the Judeans, could not bring himself to do that.

The Patience of God

But why does God permit wrong to exist, and indeed, to prosper, while it flaunts itself in His face? First of all, we need to remind ourselves that a great deal of evil is punished. Think for a moment of a world where the axiom of the Judeans was really true. "Evildoers not only prosper, but when they put God to the test, they escape." Such a world would be without a trace of love or unselfishness. Despite the horrors of evil around us, it is still clear that most evil, sooner or later, is punished. The Hitlers are destroyed. The Stalins are disgraced. It is true, "Though the mills of God grind slowly, yet they grind exceeding small" (Friedrich Von Logau, *Sinngedichte*).

Yet too many of the proud and the arrogant *do* prosper, at least in their own lifetimes. Why? Surely it is in the very character of God, who in His mercy gives every person every opportunity to find peace with Him. God received the wicked King Manasseh with open arms when he repented near the end of his life. Some of us tend to say of that, "It's not fair. Here I spend all my life denying myself and struggling to be good while that clod lives it up. In the end he repents, and I'm no better off than he is." That is exactly what the Judeans thought, and it is based on a wrong concept—that the life of faith is a dull, morbid struggle where one abstains from everything enjoyable. Ask people who are truly converted and they will tell you that they only thought they were enjoying life before. *Now* they know what enjoyment is. It is the person who repents at the end of his life who has missed living.

Another reason why God permits some evil to go unpunished is because of His justice. Jesus explained that in His parable about the wheat and the weeds (Matt. 13:24-30). To root out the weeds too suddenly would destroy much of the good wheat. So the farmer waits until the harvest to separate them. God's determination to do good to the greatest number prevents Him from carrying out swift and sudden judgment for every shortcoming. And how thankful we can be for that patience. The very Judeans who were poor-mouthing God's justice had as much reason to be thankful for that patience as did the crooks whose destruction they were clamoring for.

Those Who Feared the Lord

Not all the Jews were clamoring for the destruction of the wicked. Some of them were not responding with the cynicism of the rest of the group toward God. Some had been captured anew by the vision of the prophet. Their minds had been stirred by God's wonder and majesty. Their hearts had been captured by His love and faithfulness. And most of all, their wills had been captivated. Convinced that God's law *did* reflect His nature, certain that He was going to enforce His will on earth, persuaded that His only aim was to love His creatures, they cried out, "We will be obedient, not grudgingly or coldheartedly, but out of the glad certainty that this is life at its best."

Notice that they were called "those who feared the Lord and thought on His name." These were not simply people who cowered before the big stick in God's hand. In fact, they did not cower at all. They had put into practice the knowledge that God is Master of everything in the universe. If we really believe this, our lives will be different. If we really "think on His name" (or honor it) our behavior will be affected.

The Importance of a Name

But what does that phrase "think on His name" mean? It is important to see that Malachi uses it as a synonym for "fear the Lord." That gives us some clue right off, doesn't it? It has to do with a correct assessment of God. Yet how easily we profane the name of Jesus. And not by using it to swear with, either. No, we profane His name by making Him appear phony and empty, through phony and empty lives.

A young soldier was brought before Alexander the Great. He was charged with desertion in the face of the enemy. As the young general looked at the soldier, he saw that he was only a boy—a boy who was utterly terrified, pale and shaking. Seeing the situation, Alexander took pity on him.

"If I pardon you this time, Son, will you give me your word this will never happen again?"

"Y-y-yes, Sir!"

"Then I do so pardon you. Dismissed."

At first, the boy was stunned to immobility. But in a moment, realizing his incredible good fortune, he turned to go. As he turned, Alexander had an afterthought. "Son, what's your name?"

The boy stopped in his tracks. Slowly, he turned and stood speechless. His face, to which some color had been returning, was again as white as a snowdrift.

Alexander said, "I asked you your name, boy."

Slowly the boy stammered out, "S-s-sir, m-m-my n-n-name i-i-is—Alexander."

The general was off his raised seat and across the tent floor in a moment. Grabbing the front of the deserter's tunic, he pulled the boy's face to within inches of his own. Quietly, through clenched teeth, he said, "Son, you either change your name or change your life."

If we ever really "think on His name" which we bear, our lives will be different, bringing honor, not disgrace, to it. We will manifest Him as He is, in all His greatness and glory.

In the ancient Near East, one's name was synonymous with one's character or reputation. So Naomi, "sweetness," protested that her name ought to be changed since she had had nothing but bitterness in her life. We still use the idea of a name in somewhat that way when we say, "Bill has a good name in this community." Of course, we do not mean that the name *Bill* equals good reputation. But we have all been favorably or unfavorably disposed toward a certain name, because of some experience with a person of that name.

When we speak of God, we can equate name and character. For His name and His nature coincide perfectly. His name is *I Am who I Am* (Ex. 3:14). He is the Self-Existent, the Creator, Totally Consistent, the All-Powerful. And in the light of the promises, He is the Ever-Faithful, the Mighty-to-Bless. If the Jews had thought on His name, they would have stopped their silly games.

That truth is no less so for us Christians. Week after week we mouth Jesus' words, "Hallowed be Thy name," without more than a vague idea of what we're saying. We are asking that God's name never be dragged in the mud. We are asking that He never be made to appear a petty, nicely mannered answering service. We are asking that His importance, His power, His worth, His hair-raising presence may be manifested and recognized in every place upon this twisted, scarred earth, but especially in us. For that's what *holy* or *hallowed* means: all that God really is. To profane His name is to make Him appear less than He is.

But His name is not only *I Am*. Not any more. Ever since Bethlehem, ever since Malachi's promises were fulfilled in that obscure stable, God's name has also been *Jesus*. Jesus—Saviour, Redeemer, Friend. To think on that name seriously is to be overwhelmed. For in Jesus is revealed that divine love for which no obstacle—not even our sin—is too great. In Jesus is revealed that divine humility which would leave the courts of glory for a cattle stall in order to heal human hurt. In Jesus is revealed the divine faithfulness which would stop at nothing—even His own death—to bless us!

Duty to Each Other

The Judeans finally came to their senses. They recognized that they the creatures could not call God their Creator to account. They saw that the smallness and wretchedness of their lives was not His fault but theirs. They recognized that even if He never gave another blessing to them, He owed them nothing. But they also recognized that He longed to pour out His abundance on them, if they would stop playing God so that He could bless them.

So what did they do? Spoke to God, right? Wrong. They spoke to each other. "And the Lord gave attention and heard it" (Mal. 3:16, NASB). How strange. They spoke to each other and God answered. What was going on?

The truth which the Bible is teaching here is twofold. First of all, it is a lot easier to break a promise made to God in secret than it is to break one made before people who know us, love us, and live with us every day. For that reason, the promises we make before our brothers and sisters are often more carefully thought out. God is obviously a lot more interested in that kind of promise than in some of the off-hand, almost unconscious things we say in private prayer. This is one of the virtues of the altar call and of being baptized into a local church. Of course, these can become merely performances which are an abomination to God. Also, public profession and sharing can never take the place of secret prayer. But the serious commitment of ourselves before our brothers and sisters has an impact upon us which is difficult to break loose from.

The second truth which the Bible is teaching here is the importance of commitment to and encouragement of each other. How are you and I to genuinely sacrifice our selfish interests, our materialistic lusts, and our fears of trusting God? How are we to come into that glorious freedom of thinking of others before we think of ourselves, of finding contentment in a scaling down of our wants, and of delighting in the miraculous ordering of our daily lives? Largely through realtionships with other people.

Now please don't misunderstand me. I am not saying that horizontal humanism is the answer to our problems. Far from it! The answer to our problem is a continuous unleashing of God's Holy Spirit in our lives. Nothing less than divine power is adequate for the human problem.

But how does that continuous unleashing take place? It normally takes place through others. Karen and I have been involved in a couples group for eight years. It has been a priceless experience. Just as any group, ours is far from perfect. So if I describe it glowingly, don't think your group—or one you might organize—is a failure. Ours has consisted of about an hour of Bible study, an hour of sharing and prayer, and half an hour of dessert and laughing. Somehow when you hear a person say, "I forgive you and accept you," it's easier to hear God say it. When you hear someone else say, "Hey, I'm going through that same problem. I'm with you," it's easier to believe God is with you. When someone who cares about you says, "I'm a little troubled about this aspect of your life," it's easier to get God's perspective on our tricky self-deceptions. Somehow we think more clearly and truly and determinedly when we think outloud and together. It is easier to commit ourselves to God when we have committed ourselves to each other. And it is easier to trust God when we have come to trust each other.

Sometimes on Monday nights I am tired and discouraged, and don't want to see anybody or do anything but just sit in a chair and wallow in my depression. But Karen and I have committed ourselves to our eight brothers and sisters, and so we go. And invariably I come home lifted and helped and refreshed. Why? Because we who fear the Lord and think on His name speak together and the Lord gives attention to hear us. To keep my head on straight and my heart light in these days of danger and opportunity, I need my brothers and sisters.

Remembrance

"The Lord gave attention and heard it, and a book of remembrance was written before Him for those who fear the Lord and who esteem His name" (3:16, NASB). Surely this is one of the loveliest passages in the Scriptures. The concept of memory was very important in the Israelite faith. For only as they remembered God's acts in such a way as to influence their present choices and actions did they truly remember Him. By the same token the whole motive for living a godly life was the memory that the transcendant God had stepped into their own arena of time and space and had there manifested Himself in unmistakeable ways.

Our own Christianity has grown right out of this memory of God's acts. Jesus held up the bread and the wine and said, "Do this in memory of Me." The Lord's Supper serves as a reminder that once and for all God has revealed Himself on our level. And the memory of those historic and objective facts is the basis for all we say and do today. Take those facts away and Judeo-Christianity is one more world philosophy—one more instance of man trying to project himself upon the stars. As Paul said, "If Christ be not raised . . . we are of all men most miserable" (1 Cor. 15:17, 19, KJV). In other words, it is all a hoax. But granting the truth of those memories, then Christianity, the only fulfillment of Old Testament faith, can say, "This is the way, walk in it" (Isa. 30:21, NASB).

But there is the other side to memory as revealed here in Malachi. Not only do we remember God, but as we do, He remembers us. The thief dying on the cross whispered, "Remember me when You come in Your kingdom!" (Luke 23:42, NASB) What did he mean? Surely he was echoing the sentiments of the psalmists, for whom the worst possible fate would be to be blotted out of the mind of God (Ps. 13:1). Although they knew there was really no reason for God to remember them (Ps. 8:4), yet they dared to hope that for His own goodness sake He would keep them in the center of His mind (Ps. 25:6-7).

In God's memory all those unimportant events which have gone to make up our lives will endure forever (Ps. 112:6). Nor will God merely remember His children as a group. No, He will remember us by name. Out of all the billions who will have lived on this earth before time's final curtain, He will remember you specifically if you are His child.

Can you see the picture? Somewhere a million years from now, Gabriel is pouring over the immense roster of all who have ever lived. He comes to your name, then mine, and turns to the Father and says, "Almighty, do You remember John Oswalt?" A smile crosses that ineffable face, and in the voice which sounds like a thousand waterfalls and a thousand, thousand bells, He says, "Oh yes." And with the loving interest of a parent, He begins to recount the story of my life. He recalls a stubbed toe, a 100 on a spelling quiz, a broken heart, an inner victory about which no one ever knew. There will be only one thing missing—the record of my sins. For they are gone, gone forever.

So it will be in the day of the last battle, when good and evil stand finally arrayed against each other, all the wraps off, finally seen for what they are: the serene beauty of goodness and the gaudy tinsel of evil. Then the evil one will come to claim his spoils. He will look at you or me and say, "That one is mine, God. You know the sins he has committed. You know the rebellions he has foisted against You. He is mine. Give him to me!"

But the Father will turn to his advocate, saying, "What about it, Son?" And Jesus will look down at the gaping wounds in His hands and say, "His name is written here, Father." And God will say to the accused, "You are mine!" Then the angels will bear him away from the anguished scream of Satan, and into the bosom of the Father, who will say, "Welcome home, child."

17
ARE YOU BECOMING
MORE LIKE GOD?

"Surely the day is coming; it will burn like a furnace. All the arrogant and every evildoer will be stubble, and that day that is coming will set them on fire," says the Lord Almighty. "Not a root or a branch will be left to them. But for you who revere My name, the sun of righteousness will rise with healing in its wings. And you will go out and leap like calves released from the stall. Then you will trample down the wicked; they will be ashes under the soles of your feet on the day when I do these things," says the Lord Almighty.

"Remember the law of My servant Moses, the decrees and laws I gave him at Horeb for all Israel.

"See, I will send you the Prophet Elijah before that great and dreadful day of the Lord comes. He will turn the hearts of the fathers to their children, and the hearts of the children to their fathers; or else I will come and strike the land with a curse."

Malachi 4:1-6

The last element in the pattern, the promise of the coming One, now comes into focus again. First there is the statement of God's character. Then there is an appeal for a kind of service in keeping with that character. Then there is a response, at first of noncommitment which is manifested in all the areas of their lives, but then of commitment and worship. Finally comes the promise that God will act in the cause of justice, as He Himself sorts out the wicked and the righteous.

In this last paragraph of the book we have again, as in Malachi 3:1-5, the promise that God will come in a great day of judgment as well as of blessing. I do not want to push this too far, but it seems to me that 3:1-5 has somewhat more relevance to Christ's first coming, whereas 4:1-6 relates more to His second coming. Part of this feeling is because of the different focus of the two passages. The first relates largely to Christ's purification and judgment of the covenant people of Israel in preparation for His ministry to the world. That is the meaning of Jesus' seemingly abrupt statement to the Syro-Phoenician woman that He was sent only to the lost sheep of the house of Israel (Matt. 15:24). If He only became a worldwide miracle-worker, His mission would have been in vain. Instead, if a remnant of Israel were to be genuinely redeemed and purified, it would become the nucleus through whom the world could be reached.

Great and Terrible Day

The Second Coming of Christ will have a direct impact on all the world. His appearing will be as evident as the sunrise rather than as unassuming as the growth of a plant (Isa. 53:2). The arrogant and the proud who have strutted across the earth, apparently unpunished and unbowed, will be crying out for the mountains to fall on them to hide them from the wrath of the Lamb (Rev. 6:16-17). It will be a great and terrible day, the day of the harvest when every person will be dealt with according to his true nature.

It is important to remember that God's nature does not change in that last judgment process. His nature is, and always will be love. But the effect of His love on us is determined by *our* nature. Malachi uses the figure of the sun to express this truth (4:1-2). To the stubble, the sun is disastrous; to the wounded, it is beneficent. This figure of speech would have special impact in the Near East, where the heat of the sun is almost palpable. As the psalmist says, that heat searches out even the nooks and crannies (19:6). It is easy to imagine it sucking the last drops of moisture from the stubble, leaving it utterly dead and lifeless, as Malachi says, "without root or branch." Yet, open a putrefying wound to the sun and the same rays which destroyed the stubble will now cleanse and heal that infected place so that life, and not death, may rule.

Does the sun hate the stubble and love the wound? Well, we might put it that way, but the nature of the sun hasn't changed at all, has it? The real question lies in the nature of the thing with which the sun comes in contact. Is it compatible or incompatible with the sun's nature?

The same is true of God. Sometimes we picture the Last Judgment in this way: A sinner prostrate before God is crying out, "Please don't send me to hell, God. I never saw the error of my ways on earth but now I do. Please let me into Your heaven, God." But a hardfaced God says, "No! It's too late. You go to hell!" And the person is dragged off screaming. No wonder we ask how a good God could send anyone to hell.

But that picture is wrong. Suppose you and I were visiting a great steel mill. Just as we were passing one of the blast furnaces, its door was opened. As the breath of that roaring inferno singed our eyebrows and sucked our palates dry, our guide would say, "Just step inside for a moment, please." We would stare at him as though he had lost his mind. Step into the heart of a blast furnace? It would destroy us in an instant. No, thank you. And we would hurry away from such a crazy man as fast as we could. Does the blast furnace hate us? No, it's just that we are unprepared to endure its fiery embrace.

Why do we think that having lived our lives in such a way as to reduce ourselves to tinder-dry stubble, to crackling lifeless selfishness, we would then want to live in the midst of eternal burnings? Would we not take one look at writhing twisting tongues of flame in the midst of which He dwells and run from the azure courts of glory screaming, "Let me out of this terrible place. Anywhere but here which would destroy what I have spent my life making!"

C. S. Lewis in his book *The Great Divorce* takes this same theme and shows how those who have spent their lives honing their existence down to the single point of "I" would find any excuse to get away from the piercing reality of a heaven which invited them to final release from themselves.

The Final Healing

But the same fire which would consume a leaf in an instant would make tooled steel only the harder. Those who have spent their lives in the refining fires of God can view with ecstasy the dawning of the perfect day. For only this can bring about that final refining, that perfect union for which they have longed increasingly. Only this can bring that final healing for which they have sighed again and again. Thus, the question for you and me as we view the lightening horizon is: am I an authentic—though wounded—being, or am I making myself more and more the center of my stubbled existence?

For those who wait for the final healing, the prospect is almost too wonderful to bear. Physical infirmities will be gone; the oppression of a sinful world will be past, the tendencies of our fallen natures will no more trap us; we will experience no more frustration, guilt, or failure. It will be like being let out of jail.

Malachi compares our exultation to that of calves let out of the stall. Calves and lambs are commonly born in the winter or early spring. Consequently, many have never known anything but a dark and confining barn and barnyard. Then comes that balmy spring day when they are taken from the barnyard to a pasture which looks limitless. It is filled with lush green grass; it has the clearest, freshest water, and the pasture is decked with delicate spring flowers.

It would be a very depressed person indeed whose spirits could not be lifted by watching those calves or lambs in their newfound world— Jumping over one another, rushing here, then there, falling down for the sheer delight of rolling in that soft grass, standing still to look at the wonder of it and suddenly jumping straight up in the air for the pure joy of it. The Hebrew word for calf seems to be drawn from the verb which describes the motion of waves; rolling, bounding, crashing. And no wonder: they are free, in a world apparently made just for them. This must have been in the mind of St. Bernard of Cluny as he penned the words of his vision of heaven:

> They stand, those halls of Zion, all jubilant with song,
> and bright with many an angel, and all the martyr throng;
> the Prince is ever in them; the daylight is serene,
> The pastures of the blessed are decked in glorious sheen.

This is our heritage as children of God. Our hope is not weak or tentative. Rather, it is a glad, undergirding confidence based on the reality of Jesus' conquest of death and the witness of the Holy Spirit within us.

But we do not have to wait for death or Jesus' return to know a foretaste of this delight. In fact, if we do not know it from time to time, if there are not moments when joy comes stealing in unawares and pounces on us like a kitten jumping on its mother's tail, we are missing our inheritance. Even the calves experience those irrepressible moments. It is as if they know they are made for something better. And so it is with us. At the strangest moments, if our relationship with Jesus is intact, there will come that whisper, "You are mine." And in the midst of most serious proceedings, an idiotic smile will steal across our faces. An almost irresistible urge to clap our hands and laugh may sweep over us, and our more staid friends may accuse us of being unable to "settle down." But how else shall we respond to the heavenly intelligence? "Beloved, now are we the children of God, and it has not appeared as yet what we shall be. We know that when He appears, we shall be like Him, because we shall see Him just as He is" (1 John 3:2, NASB).

For the one who is not God's child, all unbidden an icy hand falls upon him—in the midst of the greatest hilarity or the most feverish pursuit of joy—and the whisper comes, "What's it all about? Where are you going? Why?" Perhaps the darkness lasts for but a moment before it is resolutely pushed away. Nevertheless, the fear of its return is enough to make him jam his days and nights with restless activity lest it steal in again, as it invariably will.

C. S. Lewis compared these states of mind to two people shut up in a castle. The one person knows that this is his father's house and that somewhere in the myriad rooms and corridors the father is walking. Thus every distant footfall, every echoed snatch of a song is only cause for increased delight and anticipation for the moment when they will meet.

The other person claims the castle is empty and therefore belongs to him. For him those footfalls, that music, that shadow at the end of the hallway are only cause for rising dread and the stubbornly fought certainty that, "Something is in here with me and I may encounter it at any moment." Father's house or haunted castle? Which will it be? For there *is* Someone in here with us!

Conformity to Christ

If we know that Someone is our Father, we might be tempted to live off those moments of bliss, those spiritual highs when we do not need to ask, "Where are You?" but rather can listen to Him whisper, "Here I Am." We feel His presence in an intimate personal encounter and we want to prolong it as much as possible. For us in those moments, religion is a feeling of ecstasy. But true religion is conformity to the character of God. That is why Malachi did not end his book with verse three of chapter four. Rather, he said, "In the light of this lovely certainty—the certainty of God's care for His own—come down to earth and start living out His life."

This principle is illustrated so well in the account of the Transfiguration (Mark 9:2-8). Overwhelmed by the sheer glory of the experience, Peter didn't know what to say, but, like some of us, he just had to say something. So he blurted out, "It sure feels good to be here, Lord. Let's just enshrine this great experience so we can always get this good feeling back again." I don't know whether Jesus smiled as a father does when his children say some of the silly things they do, or whether a look of pain flashed across His face. But He knew you can never get back an old feeling. If feelings are the main thing, then the next one's got to be better than the last one to satisfy. Even a second Transfiguration would not titillate like the first one.

So Jesus didn't let them build any shrines to feelings. He gave them those moments of high ecstatic feeling, because He knew that a religion without feeling is worthless. But God did not send His Son to the cross to make us feel good. He sent Him there that the marred image in us might be restored, that we might be conformed to the image of Christ.

It can hardly be coincidence that the disciples went with Jesus from the mountain of ecstasy into the valley, where they found their colleagues trying unsuccessfully to cast out a demon. It is in the valleys of our helplessness and unbelief that we see our tremendous need to be conformed to Christ.

At first Jesus' answer to the disciples' question as to why they had been unsuccessful seems baffling. He said, "This kind cannot be driven out by anything but prayer." Most manuscripts add "and fasting" (Mark 9:29, RSV). Is it possible the disciples had not prayed to ask God to drive out the demon? If they hadn't in their first flush of overconfidence, surely they must have after repeated failure. Or does this mean that some demons can be cast out without prayer? Surely not.

To me, the key is in the mention of fasting. One does not begin to fast only when the problem arises and then quit when it goes away. If fasting was not a part of the life before the problem, it will not be a valid part during the problem, either. The same is true for prayer. Praying which occurs only in the midst of difficulty is sometimes worse than none at all, because its main purpose is the manipulation of God. Faith, be it ever so vehemently pumped up during crisis, is of very little use if the tire was full of holes to begin with.

Jesus was suggesting that the disciples had not been cultivating their spiritual lives as they went along. Like Peter, they went from spiritual high to spiritual high, with a vacuum between. There was no steady discipline or self-denial, no consistent spiritual communion, no increasing conformity to the will and character of God. Thus when the crisis came, the tire was flat. And the demon was able to mock them and their powerlessness to move.

A growing conformity to the character of God is exactly what Malachi was talking about in verse four of chapter four. As we look toward that great day when all the accounts will be settled fairly, when the Son will have healed all our old wounds, we dare not forget the meaning of life here and now. To people who lived long before the first Advent Malachi said that the Messiah would come and would send a messenger, a new "Elijah" in that day, to prepare the way.

Becoming Like God

God is just and He will keep His promises. But that being so, what sort of persons ought we to be? We ought to be like God. The Apostle John spoke of our hopes of being like Christ, and then said, "Everyone who has this hope fixed on Him purifies himself, just as He is pure" (1 John 3:3, NASB). Can I make myself as pure as God? Of course not. But, if I really have the assurance that I am His child, then the consuming passion of my life will be to be like Him. If He is honest, I want to be honest. If He is true, I want to be true. If He is kind, I want to be kind. If He is love, I want to be love.

Our becoming like God is what the law is about. For the law reveals the character of God and calls those who belong to Him to live out that character in obedience and love. This is the whole thrust of Malachi's book. The prophet called his people, and calls us, to stop trying to use God for our own ends. He shows that it is folly to fault God for being unjust, when in the deepest recesses of our lives, we do not know what keeping faith really means. He challenges us to make an unreserved commitment to God and to others. He dares us to allow God at the controls of our lives, knowing that He owes us nothing. For it is there that we discover the abundance of His grace.

Where is God? At the apex of history, holding His beloved ones in His hands, drawing everything to its appointed close. But He is also *within* us, His beloved. And though He does not explain everything, the very reality of His presence becomes our earnest of that Day when the Messenger will suddenly come to His temple, never to leave it again, when the Son will rise in His glory, never to set again.